Introduction to Developmental Playtherapy
Playing and Health

Sue Jennings

Foreword by Mooli Lahad

Jessica Kingsley Publishers
London and Philadelphia

First published in the United Kingdom in 1999 by
Jessica Kingsley Publishers Ltd,
116 Pentonville Road,
London N1 9JB, England
and
325 Chestnut Street,
Philadelphia
PA 19106, USA

www.jkp.com

Copyright © 1999 Sue Jennings

Library of Congress Cataloging in Publication Data
Jennings, Sue.
Introducation to developmental playtherapy / Sue Jennings: foreword by Mooli Lahad. p.   cm.
Includes bibliographical references and index.
1. Play therapy. 2. Developmental therapy for children.
3. Child psychotherapy. I. Title.
RJ505.P6J445   1999
618.92'891653--dc21

British Library Cataloguing in Publication Data
Jennings, Sue Emmy Introduction to developmental playtherapy : playing and health : Persephone's journey 1. Play therapy I. Title
618.9'2'891653

ISBN 1–85302–635–2

Printed and Bound in Great Britain by
Athenaeum Press, Gateshead, Tyne and Wear

Coventry University

Contents

'Woman' by Noga

To my best playmates

Sophie, Harry, George, Alfie

Monster picture by Barney, aged 5

Acknowledgements

I would like to thank all my students and colleagues in Ulster, Israel, USA and Greece as well as nearer home. Everyone has been involved in workshops, research and playing around with ideas, which in turn has stimulated my creating and thinking.

There are some special people to thank individually: Ann Cattanach, Joan Walker, Galila Oren, Audrey Hillyar, Torben Marner, Robert Landy, Mooli Lahad, Gordon Wiseman, Andrew Wade.

The children who gave me pictures and told me stories are very important: Barney, Kate, Noam, Sophie, Harry, George. The picture used in the cover design is 'Five-Legged Monster', by Harry.

Sue Hall has been the most patient word-processor player, and Helen Parry at Jessica Kingsley has been fun to work with and fair in her compromises.

I want my children Andy, Ros and Hal to remember that they are dearly loved, and their partners Kath, Neil and Olga are very welcome in the family. Finally my brothers and sisters: Julia, John, Christopher and Drusilla I want to thank for special memories we shared when playing as children – especially during the latter part of the war.

Sue Emmy Jennings
Palmers Green, London 1999

Special Note to Readers

I continue to collect data from people who experiment and research with some of my basic concepts, especially EPR and the Mandala. Please send me any type of feedback on these methods, and also the questionnaires in *Introduction to Dramatherapy: Theatre and Healing* 1998, also published by Jessica Kingsley.

Foreword

I was about nine years old when this story happened. A lorry unloaded a pile of building sand in the yard of a house next to ours. At first we, the children, ignored it as we felt 'too old' for playing the sand. The builders used the pile every day and so it grew smaller and smaller. Until one afternoon a boy, who lived next door and was much 'older' than me (he was twelve), brought some old tin cars and plastic shovels and started making roads and tunnels, waterfalls and hills. Slowly, slowly, the other boys brought from the bottom of their drawers old tin cars and joined him in the game. It was past eight o'clock at night that our mothers called us home. We had a great time playing in the sand, digging, pushing, piling and playing in the fantastic world of sand, a joy that we didn't admit to for a long time. We were all covered with sand and found it a little embarrassing to admit to our parents that we 'played' in the sand pile. We tried to clean off the sand as if to hide the evidence. I can't remember if anyone paid too much attention to it. I can only reassure you that we played and played with this pile of sand until it disappeared. The day the builders finished this building was the last day of our dream-land. We never returned to play in the sand despite many other buildings that were built later in the neighbourhood.

Why did I tell you this story? Because it was when reading Sue Jennings' book about playtherapy that I returned to this secret garden. That garden was closed for years until I started working as a child psychotherapist and opened wider as soon as I had my own children and started playing with them again. It is the end of the summer and my youngest child is now turning ten. We spent some hours playing in the sand this summer and I hope it will be long before he would close that door of wondersand.

Sue's book is not only a permission to re-enter or rediscover our secret gardens, which would have been for me a 'good enough' reason to welcome it, but it is a new and in many ways a novel approach to play, playing, playfulness and drama. Sue is not confining herself to any 'big' theory. She observes, accompanies, and most of all respects the child and the child within. She is not afraid to admit to being puzzled at times or to share with us her concerns. And so she is not 'afraid' to tell us what her views are of the misleading interpretations of play by some of the 'big' names. She trusts children, as much as she trusts her inner child, and that is how she is able to communicate with them, and tell us about it. This is an introductory book and as such it has to be comprehensive; nevertheless, the book does not lose its vitality through the many quotes from therapy, poems, drama and stories together with practical examples and suggestions.

It is therefore a reader-friendly book, and although sometimes the reader may find that the stream has taken her to fantastic regions, she will discover later that she sailed in the right direction.

I would like to emphasise only one thing and that is for me the first rule of working with children: believe in what they communicate, be attentive to their stories, and learn their language. A language that for many of us got lost when the doors of the secret garden were closed behind us. Or as Sue puts it 'the tide comes in and washes it away. Things appear and then disappear'. Good luck in re-finding what was yours anyway.

Professor Mooli Lahad,
Kyriat Shmona,
November 1998

Introduction

'The Sleepy and the Beauteous'

Three-year-old George was telling me the title of a video that he wanted for his birthday and I asked him if he could remember the name, and he said 'Yes. It's called "The Sleepy and the Beauteous"'. His amalgamation of a series of images made me think of one of the essential ingredients of play. Play has its own inherent logic and this title that was probably a variation on 'The Sleeping Beauty', 'Snow White' and 'Beauty and the Beast' encapsulated George's idea of the sort of video he wanted to see.

Play and playing has for decades been considered 'a good thing' for children to be involved in, especially before they start school. Importance is given to pre-school playgroups, kindergartens, play school, play centres such as Story World and Monkey Business, which indicates that we value the development of play activity, even though it is not always clear why it is valued. The most usual answer I hear from people is 'that play develops co-ordination, motor skills and social skills'. It is rare that people tell me that play is important to develop the imagination. Indeed, sometimes the imagination is considered as something that needs to be kept under control and at times it is thought that the imagination is over-developed or that it stops the functioning of ordinary everyday life. Peter Ustinov said in a recent interview that one of his teachers told his mother: 'Peter has a highly developed imagination – which needs to be curbed at all costs.'

However, in order to develop the highest possible degree of mental functioning it is very important that the playful imagination of the right hemisphere of the brain is developed in balance with the logic, tasks and skills of the left hemisphere of the brain. Both hemispheres need stimulus and expression throughout our lives.

It is also important that we continue to acknowledge the social importance of play rather than collude with the cult of the individual.

As Gersie (1996, pp.2–3) suggests:

For young children dramatic activity and make-believe play are synonymous. Awareness of the continuities between improvised play, rehearsal and dramatic performance gradually develops as the child matures. For many adults notions of performance and play have become so inextricably linked that the very thought of re-engagement in dramatic play activity arouses complex feelings.

Whereas few children need convincing that make-believe play is a worthwhile activity, many adults (outside of visits to the theatre) cope with their fear of exposure through drama by justifying involvement in dramatic, make-believe activity in terms of some higher purpose. They say things like:

- 'the kids wanted me to join in'
- 'the simulation exercise helped me to prepare better for the job interview'
- 'it made it possible for me to understand X, with whom I otherwise just don't get on'
- 'doing drama made me understand what I find so difficult about teamwork'
- 'it made me express feelings that I have about my life that I have not said before'.

Such statements suggest that the difference between a child's and an adult's use of dramatic play does not reside in the playing itself. Children too use make-believe play to express feelings, to explore alternative approaches to situations, to prepare for difficult situations or to work though troubling thoughts. The major difference in adult and child use of make-believe play lies in the skills which are brought to the play-situation and in the conscious intent which inspires the involvement.

Society itself has been, and indeed could be again, a container for the individual, particularly with an emphasis on the culture of a society which of course includes its art and craft. Trevarthen and Logotheti (1989) point out that infants actively seek out co-operation and that this motivation is inborn:

They 'worm' culture out of their companions within a succession of special relationships that are regulated by emotion. They reason in a common cause with others and trust that social moves will assist their minds to grow freely. (p.174)

This recognition by an increasing number of writers suggests that a new appraisal is about to take place of the nature of childhood and child development, and indeed of therapeutic intervention (Jennings 1996).

The main focus of this book is to demonstrate that play, and therefore playtherapy, are necessary at a survival level and not just desirable at a functional level. I want to suggest that the capacity to play is probably biologically driven and influences species-survival. While we all need logic and knowledge to take our place in the demands of the adult world, we also need to be creative and flexible in our responses to the world, otherwise we will be trapped in repetition and rote learning which makes adaptability to new situations and unexpected happenings very difficult.

In my earlier observations of children playing which were encapsulated in *Remedial Drama* (1973) and *Play Therapy with Children* (1993) I suggested that play, especially dramatic play, is a learnt activity that happens during the first few years of any child. I now maintain that it starts much earlier, that it starts in fact in utero and develops during the life of the growing foetus. During pregnancy women spend increasing amounts of time talking to their unborn child and using their own imagination in what I term 'playful pregnancy games'. Women talk to their unborn child, and then answer themselves *as if they are the child*, so that playful dramatic interaction is in place prior to birth:

> A woman talks to the imagined child, sings to it, asks it questions, and then she answers herself AS IF she is the child. It is such a simple every-day occurrence that I had not even noticed it. You may challenge my notion that this is a dramatic interaction. However, if you observe preg-nant women talking in this way you will see that they are 'in role', using a different voice from their everyday communication; they reverse roles with the imagined child, as they answer themselves. (Jennings 1998, p.50)

My view is that after this early predisposition towards playing and drama our play emerges in developmental stages: that as one aspect of playing is achieved we move on to the next. The play method that this book describes I term **The Playtherapy Method** which is based on detailed observation of children at play.

There are many notions about developmental play which seem to fall into two main categories. There are developmental theories that are encompassed within an *orientation* such as that of Freud or Klein, or else there are pheno-menological theorists who base their notions of development on *observation* such as Piaget, Courtney and Slade.

I have serious concerns about orientation approaches to play; we have to accept an often rigid set of theories based on *interpretation*. Interpretation means we have adhered to a formula of symbol-meaning which is intended to explain intra-psychic processes.

A phenomenological approach, by contrast, is based on observations of external observable progression of play activity. It draws attention to the importance of symbol expression, but does not attach a given set of meanings to the symbols.

I give some examples of various developmental theories in Chapter 2, together with suggestions of how they in fact can get in the way of working with children rather than enhancing it. The subsequent chapters describe how the Playtherapy Method provides a solid foundation for basic play practice. It can also be directly applied with children who are damaged or distressed. The Playtherapy Method is based on observations of children's dramatic relationship with the outside world. Indeed a child develops as he or she struggle with, and conquers, the world outside. The child begins to experience the difference between everyday logic and the world of the imagination, what I refer to as *the reality of the mundane and the reality of the play* (elsewhere I call this *everyday reality and dramatic reality;* see Jennings (1990, 1992a, 1992b, 1993, 1997, 1998)).

The Playtherapy Method is based on this emerging capacity to differentiate these two realities, and on the Embodiment – Projection – Role paradigm.

During the first year of life a child's experiences are mainly sensory and physical, which I refer to as the *embodiment stage.* Slowly there is an increasing engagement with people and 'things' outside the physical world of the child which I term the *projective stage.* Children then develop the capacity for dramatising their play through a variety of roles which I term the *role stage.* Thus embodiment, projection and role, or EPR, become a basis for working in play and playtherapy.

The remainder of this book will look at the observations of play as well as the application of playtherapy in particular situations. There is also material on assessment and observation with useful recording charts for the play worker or playtherapist.

Peter Pan has to wear leaves because Captain Hook sliced off his clothes with his sword. (Harry, aged four)

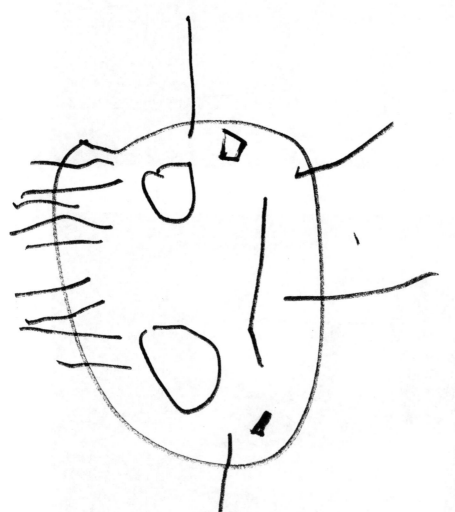

The Good Monster who is Happy by George 3½

CHAPTER I

Towards a New Philosophy of Play

Julia: And at that time I made her weep agood,
For I did play a lamentable post.

(The Two Gentlemen of Verona, IV, iv, 104)

Drama and playing are not only activities but also important developmental processes which influence the maturation and responsibility of the growing child. Some years ago I wanted to write a book entitled 'Why the British Hate Their Children' in which I wanted to draw attention to the cruelty and control that parents and institutions often impose on children. Readers will recall the uproar when the government proposed the abolition of corporal punishment in schools and physical chastisement by foster carers. People jeered at the idea that children and adolescents could sue their parents for inappropriate child rearing. The cruelty and abuse of children is projected onto child molesters and paedophiles, and such people who have already been punished are hounded across the country, as a way of distancing them from ourselves.

Alice Miller in her challenging book *For Your Own Good* (1983) suggests that various methods are used to suppress vital spontaneity in the child and she gives the examples of:

> Laying traps, lying, duplicity, subterfuge, manipulation, scare tactics, withdrawal of love, isolation, distrust, humiliation and disgrace, scorn and ridicule and forceful coercion which may even be actual torture. (p.59)

Miller describes this as 'Poisonous Pedagogy' and suggests that false information is passed on from generation to generation to young people, and that unproven adult beliefs are imposed upon them. She gives examples of untruths such as:

- a high degree of self-esteem, tenderness and strong feelings are harmful
- low self-esteem encourages a person to be altruistic
- severity and coldness are a good preparation for life.

Overall, parents are seen to be free of guilt and therefore are people who are always right. Miller points out that intimidation plays a major part in this type of child rearing and reminds us that it was very strong at the turn of the century. She points out that: 'Sigmund Freud had to conceal his discovery of sexual abuse of children by parents and instead maintain that it was the child's fantasies' (p.60).

I also maintain that we find similarly harmful projections onto the child in the theories of Melanie Klein (1932) who states that the very young infant is monstrous and destructive.

Even now we are often told that we cannot trust what children tell us, that we have to find other means of validating their experience. We are not allowed to accept that a child may communicate to us, in symbolic form, basic truths about themselves and their experience.

Children's play demonstrates their ability both to communicate and to discover their relationship with adults and the world around them

As well as play being encouraged and enhanced in a nurturing environment, children also need appropriate role models in the adults close to them. Adults provide 'the other' through which a child develops an awareness of empathy and feeling as well as appropriate ways of behaving. Therefore the child who witnesses violence in the family will be confused when their own violent mirroring is punished. If their own violence is encouraged at home as 'standing up for themselves', they will react with dismay if punished in school.

So often child rearing becomes an 'all or nothing' situation where children are completely controlled and programmed or else are given total freedom with no parental limits. What children need is a nurturing structure within which they are free to develop and explore and where certain realistic borders are placed on their day-to-day activity.

A constant dilemma is how much choice a young child should be allowed. We find many conflicts about the balance of choices between children and adults, that is, the rights of the individual. This dilemma was brought home to me in the following enchanting story which I use in my work.

In Tove Jansson's book *Tales from Moomin Valley* (1963) there is a story called 'The Hemulen Who Loved Silence'. She describes a hemulen who worked in a pleasure ground whose job it was to punch holes in tickets, so that people wouldn't have fun more than once. The hemulen had a lot of very noisy relatives who told him he should do this job because one day he would have a pension.

When he tried to explain that he wanted to be quiet his relatives tried to tell him that he was lonely and had nothing to do so he went on punching the tickets, dreaming about one day achieving the silence he longed for, and hoped he would grow old as soon as possible.

When the rains destroyed the pleasure ground, he was allowed to go and live in grandma's old park, which was like an overgrown secret garden. The hemulen had a wonderful time wading through the undergrowth and throwing his arms round trees.

> He was the owner of the moonlight on the ground, he fell in love with the most beautiful of the trees, he made wreaths of leaves and hung them around his neck. During this first night he hardly had the heart to sleep at all. (p.89)

The next day a small whomper arrived with a basket of food from the adults and said to him 'You used to punch the tickets, but if one was very small and ragged and dirty you punched beside it, and we could use it two or three times'. It turned out that all the whompers had rescued bits and scraps of the pleasure ground and they dragged them to the gates of the garden. Soon the hemulen began to reconstruct the various games. The park grew more and more fantastic and one evening it was finished. 'The sadness of completion overtook the hemulen.' (p.98)

> Mirror glass, silver and gold gleamed in the great dark trees, everything was ready and waiting – the ponds, the boats, the tunnels, the switchback, the juice stand… (p.98)

The hemulen allowed the youngsters into the park but reminded them it was a park of silence. He wondered whether they would have any fun if they weren't allowed to shout their heads off, but he could see that:

> all the park was rustling and seething with a secret and happy life. He could hear a splash, a giggle, faint thuds and thumps and padding feet everywhere. They *were* enjoying themselves. Tomorrow, thought the hemulen, tomorrow I'll tell them they may laugh and possibly even hum a little if they feel like it. (p.101)

The story ends with the hemulen going to sleep and not being worried about anything. Outside the gate of the garden, however, his uncle thinks out loud that they can't be having much fun: 'My poor relative always was a bit queer' (p.102).

What I think this story illustrates is the sadness and despair of the hemulen who was forced to join in, who wasn't allowed to state his own needs and who had the perceptions of his adult relatives imposed on him. The flood disaster enabled him at last to do what he wanted to do, which eventually did include the creation of a pleasure garden, but one that was magical and mysterious instead of being one where:

> The whirligigs whirled, the trombones trumpeted, the gaffsies and whompers and mymbles shrieked in the roller coaster every night. Edward the booble won a first prize in china smashing and all around the sad and dreamy hemulen people danced and whooped, laughed and quarrelled and ate and drank, and by and by the hemulen grew simply afraid of noisy people who were enjoying themselves. (p.18)

The theme of the secret garden where children can discover and create in their own way is central to my ideas around children's play. Slade (1954) too talks about the 'Hinterland Activity' which is activity going on for love *in an absorbed way.*

We need to remember that children need quiet times for reflection and many children play quietly, like the hemulen and maybe the Little Wooden Horse:

> I'm a quiet little horse I am, and the thought of going into the wide world breaks my heart. (*Adventures of the Little Wooden Horse*)

Frances Hodgson Burnett in her famous book, *The Secret Garden* (1911), describes in painful detail the imposition of authority onto young children. A young girl whose parents died of cholera and goes to live with a distant relative is made to feel that she must always be grateful for being given a home with her uncle. The housekeeper tells her that there is nobody to care for her and that she will have to look after herself. Having being brought up to have servants in India, then losing everything and everybody, she goes through an extraordinary culture shock when she has to do everything for herself in a strange country.

The other child in the house is bed-ridden and stunted because he is considered weak. The little girl, Mary, eventually discovers the sickly boy, Colin, and together they develop an intense friendship and are both healed by the discovery of the secret garden. The robin shows Mary where the key is and the country boy Dickon helps to make things grow and happen.

In this story the two children find their own way of blossoming and indeed they blossom as the garden blossoms.

> The place was a wilderness of autumn gold and purple and violet blue and flaming scarlet, and on every side were sheaths of late lilies standing together – lilies which were white or white and ruby. He remembered well when the first of them had been planted that just at this season of the year their late glories should reveal themselves. Late roses climbed and hung and clustered, and the sunshine deepening the hue of the yellowing trees made one feel that one stood in an embowered temple of gold. The newcomer stood silent, just as the children had done....'
> (p.298)

The stranger is Colin's father who never thought his son would be normal. He too learns from this experience, not only about his misjudgement of his son's condition, but also about what happens when an adult locks away their grief. The secret garden had originally been built for Colin's mother who died from an accident in the garden, which was why his father locked the garden away. We can see that the secret garden and the discovery of the key both unlock the father's memories and grief, with which he needs to come to terms, as well as unlocking the childlike experience of the two children through which they can grow and develop.

In my work I often use the analogy of a garden which may be secret or derelict or overgrown or scary, and together through the playing we can find the safe spaces and face the monsters and the insects.

Perhaps the attraction of so many of the gardening programmes on the television, even for non-gardeners, is some residue of a memory of a secret garden. Indeed when I was working with couples who had difficulty in conceiving, the empty garden or the idea of the womb being a garden where nothing would grow was a recurring motif. I would actively encourage the growing of a real garden, even a window box, to encourage the conception process.

However, this symbol of the secret garden is only part of the story in my philosophy of play and playtherapy. The idea of growing things in a garden and themes of cultivation and fertility are one aspect of our desires. Many people want to be 'settled cultivators' and stay in one place and grow and amass things. These are not necessarily countryside notions; all sorts of

Kate's Secret Garden

possessions can be stored and collected. Non-useful objects multiply in collections and are encouraged by the glossy magazines.

The difference between the garden and our cupboards full of collections, is the element of the seasons, the weather, and growing and dying. The ritualisation of the seasons means that even a garden is constantly moving and changing. It never stays the same.

> Another tenant now has the farm, and I a cottage – there are plenty standing empty since the plague. The garden grows the herbs I need for healing. The moon waxes and wanes. The seasons come and go .... Chill winter's bitter fingers, which had held my heart, yield to the promises of spring. Golden catkins dance once more in the Easter sun, and sap-green

hawthorn scents the air in May. Time and nature only have power to heal my hurt. Meadow-sweet and roses riot through the summer meadows, and the hay where once we lay gives place to corn. O swallows! Bring back my love! .... But they are away, and autumn's golden branches sweep like an overflowing tankard, the gutters running with froth of gold. Autumn, dark mysterious, deep, and teeming with new life. Life held by winter's spell, to come again with spring. (*Alyson, The Story of a Green Witch*, p.19)

There are many people who need to move even more and for whom the settled home base is a transitory experience in their wanderings, the home base to come back to for respite before another journey. The person who is a 'hunter-gatherer' has more difficulty in the notion of staying still or settling down, because the journey is more important. People who wander, such as Travellers, are given short shrift in our society and are often hounded from one place to the next. People are supposed to be of a 'fixed abode', proven by being on the Electoral Register. People who are nomadic are often treated with suspicion and have no status if they spurn the trappings of settling down. People in uniform such as sailors and soldiers are allowed to wander, legitimately.

We can observe in young children a tendency towards settled cultivation or wandering and it is the former that is usually rewarded in our value system. Adolescents in particular often need to wander much to the annoyance of adults and they are often described as being 'very trying'.

The *Concise Oxford Dictionary* gives several definitions of the word 'try':

- to test the qualities of a person or thing by experiment; subject to suffering of harsh treatment
- to make experiment in order to find out
- to investigate and decide
- to achieve or perform
- to smooth (as in rough surface)
- to test fit ... experimentally to see how much will be tolerated.

And there are various nautical, carpentry and rugby terms. Its roots are from Middle English and Old French. Meanings include:

Separate   Distinguish   Sift

Thus the trying time of adolescence, despite the received feelings of the adult, is an important developmental time for the adolescent where there are both active and passive processes involved; a time when there is a move towards explanations but also realisation and understanding.

Rather than seeing adolescents as 'trying', that is, testing adults in a difficult way, perhaps we can see how drama and play can allow them to try constructively, such as 'trying out' situations, exploring issues and testing given truths.

Drama and play intrinsically allow us to 'try out' before we have to make important decisions about life.

Drama and play create places where it is all right to get it wrong without fear of punishment or ridicule

We spend so much time making sure that what we do is right, that many golden poetic moments are lost and spontaneity is killed.

I was asked to give a talk to sixth-formers on careers in anthropology and dramatherapy, and I felt that an interactive approach would be more rewarding than my imparting facts and statistics. I asked the group to close their eyes and think about what they wanted to do with their lives and to try not to be influenced by what other people thought they *should* do. What was the one thing above all else they wanted to do before they died? What was their dream of life? They were asked to write this down as a piece of private information on a separate piece of paper.

They were then asked to write down what they were expected to do with their life by parents, teachers, fellow pupils and society. I then suggested they wrote down anything they felt pressured to do by these same groups. I then gave them a series of rather simplistic questions which the reader will see have an underlying theme of 'settled cultivator' and 'hunter-gatherer'.

They read through their answers then looked to see what their connections were with their 'dream of life'. They looked dismayed when they found that the thing they wanted to do most had no relation to what they were being expected to do. The questions under number 3 that gave them some possible choices began to get near some of their ideas. It then produced a lively discussion about whether one should 'follow one's nose' or train for some 'real work'. I talked about my own dream of life, going to the Malaysian rainforest with my own children, and the students were both intrigued and startled to gather that my thirteen-year-old daughter had been a midwife's assistant and helped in child delivery. Although they were interested in the experience of my own children, they were adamant that living with a tribe, learning about flora and fauna, ritual and customs, a non-competitive lifestyle and two new languages could not be classed as education. Indeed two girls suggested that I was irresponsible to remove my children from formal education and take them to the rainforest; it was reminiscent of my own elderly relatives, when they learned of my plans! Most of these sixteen-year-olds believed that a formal education would lead to a settled job, a career and a house.

The influence of the adult world – even if somewhat unrealistic – seemed already entrenched.

Sixth-Form Questionnaire

1. What is your priority when you leave school? A settled career with further education or time out to explore and perhaps travel?

2. Would you choose a job that as far as possible has a career plan to it and security or a job where the future is less certain but is flexible in its demands?

3. Choose one of the following in terms of what you would like to do:

    • work with a Nobel scientist in a laboratory that may find a cure for cancer *or* go with David Attenborough up the Amazon river to look for an unknown tribe

    • work in a flying doctor team in the outback, travelling by helicopter *or* work in a medical team in a large teaching hospital

    • serve an apprenticeship in the local garage and become skilled in car maintenance *or* work as a mechanic on a boat which travels round the world.

Influences of Others

There are several playtherapists who have influenced many of my ideas. Even though I don't necessarily agree with all of their theories, they have all made me *think*, and I now realise that several of them have gardening motifs.

Violet Oaklander (1978) has evolved a series of very specific techniques which she says 'work'. She says the basic purpose of sessions is always the following:

My goal is to help the child become aware of herself and her existence in the world. Each therapist will find his or her style in achieving that delicate balance between directing and guiding the session on the one hand and going with and following the child's lead on the other. (p.53)

She often uses drawing as a starting point which she says establishes 'self identity' and one of her most famous techniques is the 'rosebush-fantasy'. She invites the child to close his eyes, go into a space and imagine that he is a rosebush and she then asks a series of questions for the child either to tell about the rosebush, or else to draw the rosebush, for example, 'What sort of rosebush are you? How big or small are you? Do you have flowers?'. Sometimes Oaklander allows it to develop into drama when instead of telling about the picture or the fantasy, she asks the child to *be* the rosebush.

Examples:

'I'm just a little little tree hiding in the dark.
No leaves, no flowers, no nothing!'

'I'm a pretty little thing and everybody loves me. My flowers are pink and they smell lovely.'

I elaborated this rosebush technique into a story with a bird and a gardener, with trainee therapists, illustrated in the following examples.

(1) Once upon a time there was a rosebush. It was placed a bit confined between vigorous big bushes in a big garden. A gardener managed the garden. Initially he had planted the roses in a rosebed on its own around a fountain in the centre of the garden. This rosebed was surrounded by a stone 'fence' made of small round stones he had found when he had travelled all around the world.

The gardener was 63 years old, and had received a part of a garden which belonged to his rich brother who owned a huge property.

When the gardener bought the roses, he had chosen red roses. But, when he came home, he discovered that one of the rosebushes was yellow. He looked at it a bit confused, because he was sure that he had not bought any yellow bush, and he saw that all the red ones were there.

While he stood like that, suddenly a bird came flying and sat down on his shoulder. It chirped eagerly and blinked with its small eyes. Then it flew up as if it was scared by something, but was for a moment flapping in the air and as if it would have the gardener along with it, it flew against one of the corners of the garden right beside a small wrought iron gate. There it landed upon the wall that surrounded the garden and then it jumped right down on the earth beneath ... There it picked and hacked in something the gardener now discovered was an extremely fine, black and soft earth.

'Aha,' said the gardener, 'you want me to plant the yellow rosebush here?' 'Pip pip jellouu' said the bird.

Here the yellow rosebush grew up, and became higher and stronger and more beautiful than any other rosebush. In fact, soon flower experts from distant countries came to see the yellow rosebush and the earth it grew in.

'This summer, you will go and fetch your love,' said the rosebush.

'Now I want to see the ocean,' said the bird.

'Take with you a letter from me,' said the gardener. 'In it, I have put a petal from the yellow rosebush'.

(2) A rosebush aged 10 years. A gardener aged 50 years. A bird aged 5 years.

Once upon a time there was a gardener. He lived in a country east of the sun and west of the moon. He worked in a beautiful garden. He loved his work very much. In his garden there were all sorts of beautiful flowers, and he loved them all. But there was one very special rosebush he loved even more because of its rich flowering and because of the very special colours of the flowers – the colours of the sunset.

The gardener gave all his flowers a lot of care, but the rosebush got even more care.

People who passed this garden had to stop for a while. They took in this beautiful sight and the rich smell, and it filled them with joy.

People talked about this garden, and more and more came to admire it. The gardener became even more proud.

It was not only people who were attracted to this beautiful garden. There came all sorts of beautiful birds, and there was a very special and beautiful bird who became almost bewitched by the rosebush, and it decided to live in the rosebush. It was so happy there, and it was singing with its beautiful voice while the roses flowered and unfolded. It only left the rosebush for short trips to get some food and some exercise.

The people who came to enjoy the garden were filled with wonder. This was indeed a very special garden.

The gardener said, 'My life is a garden'.

The bird said, 'My life is a rosebush'.

The rosebush said, 'It is wonderful to be seen and loved'.

Although Oaklander doesn't use movement as such, she nevertheless emphasises the importance of being aware of the child's tone of voice, posture, facial expression, breathing and indeed silence. 'Silence can mean sensoring, thinking, remembering, repressions, anxiety, fear or awareness of something' (p.54).

How important it is that she emphasises the possible multiple meanings of silence, rather than the narrow idea that it is avoidance or repression. Like Slade and Sherborne, Oaklander uses the term 'flow' and suggests that the therapist can encourage flow in the child's work by being aware of his or her non-verbal cues.

By contrast, Virginia Axline describes her process of non-directive playtherapy in *Dibs In Search of Self* (1964) and *Play Therapy* (1969). Her approach is to reflect back to the child what he or she says or does and from time to time she offers interpretation based on the here and now. She warns us that playtherapy is not an imposition of desirable standards by adults onto children. She says that by taking a non-directive stance the therapist ensures that the play of the child will be child-centred and will be what the child wants to do. She has total respect for the child and total acceptance of whatever the child may offer. She says:

The therapist renders unto the child what is the child's – in this case the toys and the undirected use of them. When he plays freely and without direction, he is expressing his personality. He is experiencing a period of independent thought and action. He is releasing the feelings and attitudes that are pushing to get out into the open. (1969, p.22)

I believe that the playtherapist can establish a relationship with the child through the play. The playtherapist in any case provides a structure so that no therapy can be termed completely non-directive. Children will direct me in terms of activities they want me to do and roles that they want me to play.

There are several gardening motifs in the work of sand playtherapists. Most of us have played in the sand on the beach both as child and adult. We have created landscapes, castles with moats decorated with shells and seaweed. We have written our name, dug deep holes and filled them with water. We have allowed ourselves to be buried and trickled sand on sleeping friends. Whatever we have created, the tide comes in and washes it away. Things appear and then disappear.

People will recall the moving scenes of Derek Jarman's last years as he created beach sculptures near his house at Sellafield: endless shapes and patterns and constellations made from things he found on the beach.

Sand play and therapy was pioneered by Margaret Lowenfeld in her book *Play in Childhood* (1935). She developed what she called 'World Technique' for children to express their inner world through toys in a sand tray. She used a very wide range of objects: natural materials, people and animals of all sorts of sizes, cars, trains and so on. She also emphasised the importance of sand, as well as sand and water, in stimulating a wide variety of landscapes and seascapes, and in tunnel making. She thought that the tactile experience of the sand in its wet and dry form was also important. I have a lot of respect for Margaret Lowenfeld's ideas, and totally agree with her when she expresses a disbelief in the importance of transference in psychotherapy. She puts the emphasis on the children themselves and the sand play helping them to discover positive aspects of their personalities.

Dora M. Kalff (1980) is a Jungian child psychotherapist who works through sand play. She describes the stages of first 'mother–child unity' where the child's experiences are of total safety and security. After one year, the self of the child separates from the mother and a relationship of trust develops between the mother and infant. The third phase manifests itself at the end of the second year which, Kalff says, is the stabilisation of the unconscious. It is expressed through play, drawing and painting and the ancient language of symbols such as circles and squares and human figures of 'Godly content'. She writes, 'We accept the validity of these symbols of the wholeness of the human psyche because they have occurred everywhere without exception from the earliest times of man' (p.24).

She discusses the emergence of a healthy ego which can only develop from a basis of complete security. If it hasn't emerged between two and three years of age it can be 'recovered' in therapy especially through sand play.

Kalff states that in the first stage of ego development pictures of animals and vegetation predominate. In the next stage there are battles which go on repeating themselves, but she suggests that the child is strengthened so that he or she can take up battles with external influences and overcome them. Like Lowenfeld, Kalff emphasises the importance of having a variety of materials and also stresses the importance of the size of the sand box; it should be the right size for the eye to encompass. She describes it as a space that should be both free and protected.

I have many difficulties with Jungian theory and in my anthropological work have not found any evidence of a collective unconscious or even an indication that there are similar cross-cultural symbols in child and adult development. Jung, like Freud, put forward a total theory of the human psyche, in which we have to accept certain major givens. Now that we know much more about Jung's early influences, and the fact that he hijacked ideas from his patients and wrote them up as his own, gives me a healthy scepticism towards his creed.

So much of what we do and create is culture-specific and influenced by the value system around us, that I think it is dangerous to make assumptions about universality: for example the universality of symbols and their meaning. I shall talk about the influence of the therapist on a child in subsequent chapters but there is no doubt that the form and structure of the therapy influences both what people say and what they dream. Nothing that we do, awake or asleep, is free from our surrounding influences. **The influence of therapists is often as strong, if not stronger, than the influence of parents**.

The work of two of my contemporaries, namely Ann Cattanach (1993, 1994, 1997) and Mooli Lahad (1987, 1992), has had a profound influence on my thinking and practice in playtherapy. Cattanach is one of the most experienced people using playtherapy, both in assessment and in clinical intervention, with children who have been sexually abused.

Her approach is down-to-earth and focused and she spends a lot of time in helping the child to construct narrative stories, which is well illustrated in the following example:

> And there is even hope for change from the monsters, at least in a story! We need to contain that lost uncle who went to prison and now is – where?

The Bad-Tempered Dinosaur

> There was once a very bad-tempered dinosaur locked up in a cage.
> And the guard said: 'Shut up, can't you see no one liked you?'
> Dinosaur didn't like that at all.
> So he used all his strength and managed to get out of the cage.
> Everyone started running and the dinosaur even picked up a big car and threw it and it hit the guard and squashed him.
> The police car came and put on the siren.
> Dinosaurs don't like that noise and he ran away screaming and quickly went back to his cage.
> And he was good for ever and ever.
> So everyone began to like him and he had some friends. He got fed every day.
> And he even got a bigger cage. (Cattanach 1997, p.107)

She usually takes her playtherapy to the child and uses a blue carpet to contain and set borders on the playtherapy experience. In her several books on playtherapy practice, which have an enormous range of methods, she comprehensively describes the equipment she uses, for example:

> I always bring a variety of play dough and tactile material for modelling, smelling and touching, and some jelly like sticky worms and sticky balls which can be touched, ripped up and generally used in whatever way the children think fit. (1992, p.64)

Mooli Lahad (1992) has immense experience of working with children who are stressed or who have been abused. He has evolved a multi-model which considers the coping mechanisms that the child already possesses. It is based on 'The Six-Part Story Making' in which the child draws a story in six parts with the following elements.

1. Main character, hero or heroine.
2. The main character's task or mission.

3.   Who or what helps the main character?

4.   Who or what are obstacles to prevent the task being accomplished?

5.   How does the character deal with the obstacle?

6.   Then what happens?

He says that the therapist must listen on several levels, for example the tone in which the story is told after it has been drawn, the context of the story and its messages. The therapist is able to observe the coping modes of the story which come under the headings of: Belief, Affect, Social, Imagination, Cognition, Physical; that is, BASIC Ph. This is illustrated in the following diagram.

Lahad emphasises that the BASIC Ph assesses understanding, coping and resilience.

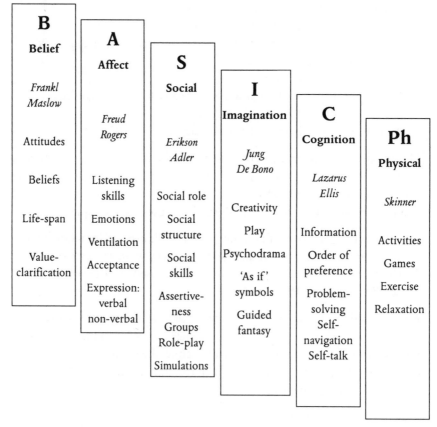

Figure 1.1 Lahad's BASIC Ph

Stressful situations become unbearable when they are prolonged, and we are no longer capable, using the resources at our disposal, to be rid of or to lessen the stress. Under circumstances where repeated attempts do not avail, the situation could turn into a crisis. Many times a situation becomes a crisis because the individual uses 'more of the same thing' to be rid of the stress; in other words, a person becomes set in the mould, using the same mode of coping endlessly, neither progressing nor changing anything. In this case the crisis stems from being stuck or from inflexibility on a primary prevention level. My 'multi model approach' aims to teach the individual a number of different options in order to gain the flexibility in coping with stressful situations, rather than reaching a dead end. (Lahad 1992, pp.154–155)

What I like about Lahad's approach is that it emphasises the health of the child and not the problems. He looks for ways in which the child's strengths can be enhanced rather than the weaknesses emphasised. As I described earlier, this method maximises the child's choices within a structured framework. As well as being used as a playtherapy intervention the BASIC Ph and 'The Six-Part Story Making' (6PSM) can be used in diagnosis and assessment.

My own philosophy of work with children may not be very new, but it brings together in a new coalition various influences from practitioners, theoreticians and the world of the arts, and makes them into a working frame of reference. It is based on a belief that children need to be heard, accepted and respected. It is based on a foundation that play and drama are already given when a child is born and are primary processes rather than secondary learnt processes. Children play in order to discover and make statements about their world, as well as encompassing the ritualisation of both pleasurable sound and movement and frightening episodes. It seems obvious, therefore, that this should form a basis in order to practise playtherapy. The Playtherapy Method based on the three stages of Embodiment, Projection and Role (EPR) provides a formulaic but flexible means of realising playtherapy practice.

By the end of this book, we shall see that not only do children structure their lives and playing with EPR, but we are also strongly influenced by EPR in our adult lives. Our ultimate choice of occupation is influenced by whether we feel more at ease in physical work, projected work or dramatic work (see Jennings 1998).

George, aged three, is having a private phone conversation on a toy phone, where he is talking to his mother and answering himself as if he is her. When he speaks as his mother he puts his head on one side.

'Hello Mummy.'
'Hello.'
'When are you coming home?'
'Later.'
'What, now?'
'No, later, after you're asleep.'

CHAPTER 2

Some Developmental Theories

Hamlet: The play's the thing
         Wherein I'll catch the conscience of the King.

(Hamlet, II, ii, 603)

In this chapter I shall consider some of the theories of human development. We will start with those I find most helpful and finish with those that I feel can get in the way of playing with children.

It is only comparatively recently that ideas from play and drama have begun to be integrated into therapeutic approaches with children, and it is a slow beginning. There seems to be an issue when we refer to these processes as 'artistic' because within our current social convention if something is 'artistic' then it cannot be 'scientific'. Many theorists claim that their developmental work is scientific, meaning that it can be observed and measured.

> Scientists often take the line that whatever cannot be proved by means of the usual scientific methods are matters that should not be raised at all. Yet only by asking such questions, even if at present we are unable to answer them, can we think about a direction in which to take our inquiries. They stretch our imaginations, and that is always a useful exercise. Some of what I write about will be from observation, but some will be pure speculation. How often has yesterday's speculation become today's fact? (*Dogs Never Lie About Love,* p.18)

All play can be observed and measured, even though we might prefer to term it artistic. However, observation, although it is influenced by the eyes, ears and value system of the observer, nevertheless does not have to infer meaning or give interpretations on the phenomena. Interpretation can close exploration rather than encourage it.

In the Embodiment stage of development I have found the ideas of Veronica Sherborne (1975, 1990) extremely helpful. She emphasises the importance of children experiencing their body as a whole body before they become aware of the individual body parts. Sherborne's ideas in movement and physical activity are very useful for the playtherapist and she emphasises the importance of the adult human body for the child to work against. She suggests that children need the experience of 'working with' another body as well as 'working against', which contribute to the development of the 'we' identity and the 'I' identity. She emphasises the development of trust which is first experienced through the body when a child is held and rocked, and later in movement work, when a child balances, or jumps to be caught and knows that the adult will be there. The child develops a sense of both trusting their self and trusting the other. Sherborne describes in her books and also illustrates in her several films a range of physical activities that can be practised by the play leader or playtherapist.

I am reminded of George's description of 'The Sleepy and the Beauteous' when I look at the work of Peter Slade, which he published in his ground-breaking book *Child Drama* (1954). Slade talks about the enjoyment experienced by the child in play and uses terms such as:

> Happiness-development: a stage in creative expression aimed at by the teacher. First signs of joy dependent on an out-flow.

> Hinterland-activity: activity going on for love, in an absorbed fashion, even when some other players are purposely in view. A natural development which takes place from time to time amongst children.

> Out-flow: the pouring out of creative forms of expression, a tendency which can be regulated and encouraged, and which by frequent opportunity becomes a habit promoting confidence.

In the above points Slade draws our attention to the joyousness of play and the absorption of play activity. He states unequivocally the important idea that play promotes confidence. Indeed, we have all observed children who are too timid to commit themselves to play and need very sensitive invitations from other children or adults in order to participate in play activity. Slade refuses to be rigid about developmental stages but suggests the following are useful for observation:

- *0 – 3 ½ years*: peep-bo, sense trials (circle appears), art forms (including less obvious music and drama), the game, trials leading to play

- *3 ½ – 4 years*: play proper and rhythm established (circle continues but properties abandoned)

- *5 years*: dramatic play

- *6 years*: the dawn of seriousness

- *6 ½ years*: the glorious years

- *9 years*: plays created without aid (a further dawning of responsibility; the circle still continues).

In the above it is important for us to see that the playing includes art forms, what I refer to as 'proto-art'. By the age of four years old, where Slade suggests that properties are abandoned I would suggest, in other words, that the child moves from projective playing with 'things' to dramatic playing, through roles and characters.

Slade also draws our attention to the child slowly being able to discern good and evil together with an awareness of society, when he talks about 'the dawn of seriousness'. Indeed I would suggest that during these early years the child is developing a conscience and is becoming aware of the outcome of their actions. I would go further and suggest that for some people with personality disorders, who may have psychopathic personalities, this development of conscience through play has not occurred at an early age.

Once we start to experience as a child the ability to be 'other' (and as we see this starts with our being able to talk to the toy and then role-reverse with it), we are able to go beyond self and the needs of the self. We experience the beginnings of conscience which means that we begin to understand some form of moral code; that is, we start to know the difference between 'good and bad' or 'right and wrong'. It may be considered very old-fashioned to use this type of language and even to consider the notion of a moral code. However, I maintain that everything we do is underpinned by a belief system or ethical principles. Usually these have evolved collectively and not individually, because they have been found to work, in other words they make it possible for the individuals in a society to lead their lives reasonably effectively. Just because some systems of belief or ideology have been abused and certain groups of people have suffered oppression, is not to say that an ethical code does not work. I do not believe that we are helped by the view that as long as it feels right for me then it must be all right. Sometimes therapy is described as 'sorting out myself', and I have talked earlier about how, in individual therapy, a person can be 'sorted out' at the expense of others (Jennings, 1995), and often to their detriment. Again and again, I come back to this view that individuals exist in relation to others, and that any impact on one will have an impact on the others. At the very least, the 'confessional' took into account the context and the code, which are not usually present in psychotherapy.

Richard Courtney (1982) has written extensively on his observations of the dramatic development of children. He emphasises the capacity for the child to act 'as if he is another' which comes from empathy, identification and imitation. He suggests that when a child can **experience the other**, then he or she is able to take on the role of the other. He divides play activity into the following stages:

- *0 – 10 months:* impersonatory stage
- *10 months:* the Primal Act; ability to act 'as if'
- *1 – 2 years:* symbolic play
- *2 – 3 years:* sequential play
- *3 – 4 years:* exploratory play
- *4 – 5 years:* expansive play
- *5 – 7 years:* flexible play.

It is interesting that Courtney (1982, p.13) emphasises the 'as if' in the child's development, which as I said earlier is influenced by the mother being able to role-reverse or play 'as if' she is the child (Jennings 1998). By being able to play the role of 'the other' we are able to have some understanding of 'the other' which forms a very important basis for social development.

Sara Smilansky (1968) identified six evaluating factors in relation to sociodramatic play. She makes use of these in observation of children's play both before and after play intervention to test whether change has taken place:

1. Imitative role-play – the child undertakes a make-believe role and expresses it in imitative action and/or verbalisation

2. Make-believe in regard to objects – movements or verbal declarations are substituted for real objects

3. Make-believe in regard to actions and situations – verbal descriptions are substituted for actions and situations

4. Persistence – the child persists in a play episode for at least ten minutes

5. Interaction – there are at least two players interacting in the framework of the play episode

6. Verbal communication – there is some verbal interaction related to the play episode.

Smilansky emphasises the difference between sociodramatic play (or social dramatic play) and play with rules, and suggests that they are two separate psychological systems. According to her observations, children may engage in play with rules and be unable to participate in sociodramatic play.

Whereas the above descriptions of the development of play and drama expand our understanding of the child's world, the psycho analytic stages I find less helpful and indeed limiting and reductionist.

Freud's Eight Stages (Rycroft 1985)

- *0 – 1 years*: Oral-sensory
- *1 – 3 years*: Muscular-anal
- *3 – 5 years*: Locomotor-genital (Phallic-Oedipal)
- *6 – puberty*: Latency
- Puberty and adolescence
- Young adulthood-genitality
- Adulthood
- Maturity.

Freud's theory emphasises psychosexual development and gratification of needs. He suggests that the libidinal sexual drives are primary processes without control or boundary, illustrating what he calls 'the pleasure principle'. These are antagonistic to secondary processes of logic and rational thought which control the primary processes. The 'pleasure principle' contrasts with the 'reality principle' governed by the demands of an outside world.

Freud (1922) of course suggests that the 'id, the ego and the super-ego' mediate the relationship between primary and secondary processes and the inner and outer life. He says that a child cannot separate the healthy life-regulating 'ego' from the pleasure-seeking instinctual 'id' until he or she has moved through the oral, anal and phallic stages.

In my own observations of child development I find no basis for Freud's Oedipal theory and indeed find it an unhelpful transposition of selected parts of an Ancient Greek myth to a distorted perception of a child's maturation. I am considered a heretic for suggesting that this adult assumption about a child's behaviour may be invalid. This assumption is made by a man, moreover, who ignored the *reality* of child sexual abuse.

One version of the Oedipus story is as follows:

> Laius had been warned by Apollo's oracle that the son born to Jocasta would kill him. The baby was therefore exposed on Mount Cithaeron, with its ankles pierced by a long pin, but was rescued by a shepherd from Corinth who took him to his king, Polybus. Oedipus was brought up in Corinth as son and heir to Polybus. He was taunted for resembling neither of his parents and went to Delphi for reassurance. The oracle told him he would kill his father and marry his mother, so he decided not to return to Corinth. He travelled alone towards Thebes, met Laius at a narrow crossroads, and killed him. He went on to Thebes, rid the people of the Sphinx, was acclaimed king and married Laius's widow, his mother. Their four children: Antigone, Ismene, Eteocles and Polynices. Some years later, Thebes suffered from a plague which the oracle said could only be removed if the murderer of Laius was driven out of the country. By his resolute investigations Oedipus finds out the truth, blinds himself in horror, and is led into exile by his daughter Antigone. He reaches Colonus in Attica after years of wandering, is given sanctuary by Theseus of Athens, and mysteriously disappears in a sacred grove. (Radice 1971, p.177)

There are other references to the Oedipus story in classical literature. For example:

> In the *Odyssey* Oedipus is mentioned as the son of Laius, king of Thebes, who has the misfortune, through ignorance, to marry his mother; when the truth came out she hanged herself, but he continued to reign in Thebes…. The *Iliad* adds briefly that he was eventually killed in battle and buried with military honours. There is no mention of an oracle. It was doubtless the lost epic *Thebais* which was the source for the later concept of Oedipus as a polluted outcast, burdened with his guilt, and also for the working out of the curse of the House of Labdacus. (Radice 1971, p.177)

I have used the Oedipus story in many playtherapy and dramatherapy workshops and the following themes are the ones that move people the most: first, the news from the Oracle when Lains and Jocasta learn about their destiny as parents. It has many parallels in contemporary life when couples wonder whether or not to have children, if, for example, there is a history of mental illness in the family or hereditary disease. Second, many participants relate to the scene where the baby is abandoned with wounded feet and is later rescued by a shepherd. Third, when Oedipus is blind and begins to see or understand at a deeper level.

What I find more interesting and significant in this story are the following:

- even abandoned babies are rescued (compare with Shakepeare's *The Winter's Tale*)

- bullying of adopted children because they don't look like their parents

- Oedipus' 'road rage' when he kills an old man at a crossroads (who turns out to be his father)

- blindness can enable seeing at a deeper level (compare with Shakespeare's *King Lear*).

In *The Winter's Tale*, the Queen's (Hermione's) child is abandoned on the orders of the King (Leontes) and is discovered by shepherds. Eventually the family is reunited after the King's remorse over his treatment of his wife. We are drawn to the rustic image of the good shepherd contrasted with the complicated and often cruel life of the court. Similarly in Oedipus, the shepherd discovers the 'lost sheep' – the baby has cruelly been abandoned with a metal pin between his feet – hence his name, Oedipus – swollen-foot.

In *King Lear* the theme of eyes – blindness – seeing – are all motifs and metaphors throughout the play. However the most dramatic scene is when Gloucester has his eyes put out by two of Lear's daughters and son-in-law. Later he meets Lear whose mind is wandering:

Lear: I remember thine eyes well enough. Dost thou squiny at me? No, do thy worst, blind Cupid; I'll not love. Read thou this challenge; mark but the penning of it.

Gloucester: Were all thy letters suns, I could not see.

Edgar (aside): I would not take this from report. It is;
And my heart breaks at it.

Lear: Read.

Gloucester: What, with the case of eyes?

Lear: O, ho, are you there with me? No eyes in your head, nor no money in your purse? Your eyes are in a heavy case, your purse in a light; yet you see how this world goes.

Gloucester: I see it feelingly.

Lear: What, art mad? A man may see how this world goes with no
eyes.
Look with thine ears.

(King Lear, IV, v, 137–152)

Myths and stories and great texts such as Shakespeare and the Ancient Greek
plays are very important materials for use in playtherapy and dramatherapy.
They are the big story within which we can discover our personal story but
the important thing is that they create a **dramatic distance** which enables
therapeutic work to take place. By abolishing the distance like Freud and may
others, and directly applying the myths to everyday life, we produce an
amputated experience out of the context of the whole story. Look how much
richer is the metaphoric language when we go back to sources.

Melanie Klein (1932) rejected Freud's ideas of libidinal development and
claimed that the infant navigates a succession of introjections and
projections. These are 'feelings' and 'wishes' that are internalised from the
outside world or externalised in the inside world of the infant. She believes
that the first position or stage is paranoid-schizoid in which the infant splits
the experience of the good and bad breast: introjecting the good breast and
projecting the bad breast.

> Her theory stresses the innate ambivalence between love and hate which,
> she maintains, derives from this basic opposition. She sees the destructive
> drives, sadism and aggression of the infant as being a defensive turning
> away from the self of this inherent, self-destructive death instinct. She
> focuses on how the infant supposedly copes with its overbearing
> instinctual drives in relation to the mother and her breast. But, for Klein,
> the infant emerges as truly monstrous, possessed by 'fantasies' of sadistic
> destruction directed towards the mother's body. (Rycroft 1985 p.15)

She suggests that the infant is truly monstrous with fantasies of destruction
towards the mother's body which are accompanied by persecutory anxieties
as early as a few months old. She interprets sucking and biting as illustrative
of the innate ambivalence between love and hate or indeed life and death
instincts of the child. She says the infant struggles with both itself and its
mother as being both loving and destructive objects. Her second phase, the
'depressive position' comes after four months and stays for the rest of the first

year, in which the synthesis of good and bad produces depressive anxiety. Guilt emerges about destructive feelings towards the good mother.

Both Freud and Klein used 'instinctual theories' as a basis for their work which nowadays is usually described as 'object relations' theory. With Klein's work again I find an adult projection onto the infant of adult fantasies rather than the other way round and I am reminded of the work of Dickens in *Oliver Twist* and *Great Expectations* where children are perceived as monstrous and in need of starvation and beating.

> 'Oh, you little wretch!' screamed Charlotte, seizing Oliver with her utmost force, which was about equal to that of a moderately strong man in particularly good training, 'Oh, you little un-grate-ful, mur-de-rous, hor-rid villain!' And between every syllable, Charlotte gave Oliver a blow

'Oliver plucks up a spirit', by George Cruickshank, from Charles Dickens' Oliver Twist

with all her might: accompanying it with a scream, for the benefit of society. (*Oliver Twist* 1987, p.88)

Children were not encouraged to ask questions, it was a question of 'ask no questions and I'll tell you no lies'.

'Answer him one question, and he'll ask you a dozen directly. Hulks are prison-ships, right 'cross th' meshes.' We always used that name for marshes in our country.

'I wonder who's put into prison-ships, and why they're put there?' said I, in a general way, and with quiet desperation.

¹   *(Great Expectations 1994, p.16)*

Psychoanalytic thinking has moved from the purely instinctual theory to a more developed 'object relations' theory in which the relationship between objects has been given more prominence through the work of people such as Ferenczi, Balint, Winnicott and Guntrip (Rycroft 1985). Nevertheless, they still operate reductionist interpretation within a closed system of symbols.

Indeed, when Anna Freud, who was analysed by her father, worked with children, she maintained that if a child rejected an interpretation, it meant it was true!

Winnicott's theories (1974), which will also be referred to later in the discussions on playtherapy, are embedded in a classical Freudian framework and they draw attention to the series of relationships that the child forms, for example:

1.   Mother's love expressed physically

2.   Mother's holding of a child in unintegrated state

3.   Mother and child in two-person relationship

4.   Mother, father and child in triangular relationship.

According to Winnicott, in adequate surroundings, mothers go through a phase of 'primary maternal preoccupation' (Winnicott 1975), which is similar to falling in love, a mother's primary occupation being to satisfy the child's needs. As the mother's other interests return, this assists the child to develop a balance between satisfaction and frustration so that the child moves from being held by the mother in an unintegrated state, to a two-person relationship of mother and child, and then to the triangular relationship of the family. The child is then able to deal with more maturing relationships with siblings and other people outside the family.

Winnicott's unique contribution to the object relations theory is the identification of what he terms 'transitional phenomena'. He believes that the child is assisted in its separation from the mother through phenomena that come to represent the mother, her presence, love and care, such as the 'security blanket' and, later, soft toys. Winnicott has observed that transitional phenomena act as a defence against anxiety between the ages of four and twelve months, where soft material is sucked, caressed, often accompanied by 'mum-mum' sounds. We shall look further at transitional phenomena and their relationship with early play activity later in this chapter.

Although Klein introduced the technique of play through which interpretations could be made about a child's unconscious world, it was Winnicott who recognised the importance of the playful and creative *relationship* between mother and child, and between therapist and client. Both however fit within the object relations theoretical framework in relation to child development.

Carl Jung's theories have only been applied to work with children in recent years, in particular through the pioneering work of Michael Fordham (1986). Fordham suggests that the process of deintigration and reintegration is an archetypal one, not belonging to myths as such but instead being 'much more primitive'. He suggests that the infant's ego is not sufficiently developed to differentiate between archetypal and real objects. Fordham suggests that care must be taken with the belief of the mythic 'ideal stage' which is like a state of total bliss. This was written about by Neumann (1973) when he postulated three stages of ego development. The 'animal, vegetative stage, fighting stage, the adaptation to the collective'. Fordham suggests that Neumann's writing is poetic but obscured by the application of the system derived from mythology 'to such an extent that there is not reference to a real child from start to finish of his book' (1986, p.27).

I must confess that I find Fordham's scepticism towards the idea of the mythic child applicable to so much theorising about children. Indeed, when I was conducting my own field research with the Temiar people of Malaysia I came across extensive writing concerning their 'dream culture'. There were detailed descriptions of how Temiar children are socialised through their dreams at after-breakfast dream clinics. I found no evidence of these practices during my research and can't help but feel that western people have this need to project ideal types onto tribal societies and children or else invent mythical images such as monsters to describe children. However Temiar children and adults regularly play in many forms:

> Most of the children's play is imitation of adult life, including the dance and trance sessions. Sometimes these will be imitations of actual sessions that have happened the previous evening. Sometimes the children will spontaneously devise their own. I refer to such behaviour as playing-at-seance. These play sessions happen outside or in a corner of the house. Children use small pieces of bamboo to imitate the stompers and they will dance and sing and sometimes imitate the giddiness of the trance beha viour. Occasionally a young adult, will join in and show them rhythms and tune. However, if the playing becomes too loud and obtrusive, older people are quick to tell them to calm down. Parents were insistent on obedience to behaviour governed by cosmic rules, even though children did not always take them too seriously. In this way children were being taught to control their spontaneous play.
>
> As well as play, spontaneous playful dancing and singing sessions also occur among adults in the house in the evenings. These can involve anyone who happens to be in the village, even foreigners. There is usually little, if any, preparation and decoration for an adult play-dance. It may start with a small group getting together and singing, others gradually joining in. There is an atmosphere of lightheartedness and fun. Sometimes trancing is involved in a spontaneous form among young people, when it is regarded essential as play. Sometimes older people will come and watch; again they will also bring the playing to a halt if they think it is getting out of hand. For example, if there was screaming and shouting to a rhythm beat on a metal tray, an older man or woman would tell them curtly to calm down, to do it 'properly', sometimes demonstrating a rhythm. (Jennings 1995c, p.69)

Psychosocial Development

Erikson, although considered by many clinicians to have contributed to the understanding of object relations theory, nevertheless places unique emphasis on the importance of social development. According to Kernberg (1984), Erikson does not differentiate between the organisation of self-representations and object-representations, and according to Jacobson (1964) he 'moves in a direction of a sociological conceptualisation of ego identity'.

Erikson's epigenetic chart (1977, p.245) places his eight own developmental stages alongside those of Freud:

1. Basic trust versus mistrust: 0 – 1 years

2. Autonomy versus shame and doubt: 1 – 3 years

3. Initiative versus guilt: 3 – 5 years

4. Industry versus inferiority: 6 years

5. Identity versus role confusion: adolescence

6. Intimacy versus isolation: young/adulthood

7. Generativity versus stagnation: middle age

8. Ego integrity versus despair: old age.

Erikson was interested in the conflicts and crises that arise when these stages do not flow easily into one another – as is frequently the case. It is important to note that although Erikson saw these stages as eight discrete steps, nevertheless he said they must all exist in some form or other from the beginning, as 'each comes to its ascendance, meets its crisis, and finds its lasting solution during the stage indicated' (p.246). Erikson claims that his analysis stands for all societies and for all people.

Anthropologists, myself included, would question the western notion of imposing universality onto differing (especially non-western) culture.

Piaget's Observation of Intellectual Development

Piaget's work has had a profound influence on both educationalists and psychologists (Piaget 1962). Piaget repeatedly investigated how children adjust intellectually to the world in which they live and he identified four stages in the development of cognition:

1. Sensorimotor: 0 – 2 years

2. Pre-operational: 2 – 7 years

3. Concrete operations: 7 – 11 years

4. Formal operations: 11 years onwards.

In terms of play, this represents an important move from Stage 1 – which includes the discovery of the relationship between sensations and motor behaviour; 'object constancy' – knowing something exists when it cannot be seen – to Stage 2 – which is the capacity to employ symbols, especially in language, to portray the external world. Within this stage, Piaget claims that the child is egocentric, that is he can only grasp that his point of view is possible. Stage 3 is concerned with logic and maths and Stage 4 with abstract thinking. Critics of Piaget suggest that he neglects feelings in this pursuit of intellect and pays little attention to the arts in contrast to science and maths. However, within its limitations in relation to childhood anxieties and dreams, it nevertheless forms an important aspect of the potential for the multi-model approach.

According to Lahad (1992), for example, a child may be able to cope in the logical sphere of operations but they may not have coping skills in the affective areas. This would indicate that the logical sphere would form a basis for initial therapeutic work.

This chapter summarises, selectively and briefly, various theorists who put forward developmental models of theory and practice. These include the drama and play people, object relation theorists, Jungian sand play practitioners as well as the psychosocial and intellectual theorists. These have formed the backdrop against which my own developmental observations have emerged – Embodiment, Project, Role. However, no developmental statement is complete without one of the originals – William Shakespeare.

> *Jaques:* All the world's a stage,
> And all the men and women merely players;
> They have their exits and their entrances,
> And one man in his time plays many parts,
> His Acts being seven ages. At first the infant,
> Mewling and puling in the nurse's arms;
> Then, the whining schoolboy, with his satchel
> And shining morning face, creeping like snail
> Unwillingly to school; and then the lover,
> Sighing like furnace, with a woeful ballad
> Made to his mistress' eyebrow; then, a solder,
> Full of strange oaths, and bearded like the pard,
> Jealous in honour, sudden and quick in quarrel,
> Seeking the bubble reputation
> Even in the cannon's mouth; and then, the justice,
> In fair round belly, with good capon lined,
> With eyes severe, and beard of formal cut,
> Full of wise saws and modern instances,
> And so he plays his part; the sixth age shifts

Into the lean and slippered pantaloon,
With spectacles on nose and pouch on side,
His youthful hose, well saved, a world too wide
For his shrunk shank, and his big manly voice,
Turning again toward childish treble, pipes
And whistles in his sound; last Scene of all,
That ends this strange eventful history,
In second childishness, and mere oblivion,
Sans teeth, sans eyes, sans taste, sans everything.

(*As You Like It,* II, vii, 140–167)

Meanwhile let us move on to consider several theories of playtherapy as such in order to understand our endeavour more fully.

'I've got a secret. It's door.' (George, aged three)

Me – and me – and me

CHAPTER 3

The Playtherapy Method

'You cannot be serious!'

(Said in the middle of a game by John MacInroe)

In Chapter 2 we saw that writers such as Slade who emphasise joyous dramatic activity and Courtney who describes the 'Primal Act', take seriously the spontaneous playfulness of children. They do not try to imbue it with adult projections and interpretations. Courtney (1982) suggests that: 'Drama provides the *felt* basis for rational thought' (p.17).

My primary goals in playtherapy are:

- to reskill and empower children through playtherapy in order for them to live life in a fulfilled manner

- to maximise their play functioning which will enable self-healing processes and promote greater well-being.

In dramatic playing children find resolutions, challenge reality, invent worlds and develop their imagination usually within the protected world of grown-ups. Many parents and teachers will have helped to encourage children's play and are often called in as an arbiter in the play and games of young children.

Early Markers of Life Stages

Embodiment – Projection – Role are the **markers** of life changes which are ritualised through playing and drama from one stage to the next. We can see how the child's early experiences are physicalised and are mainly expressed through bodily stimulus and the senses. This is the **Embodiment** stage where the physicality of play is predominant. It is through these physical experiences that the child develops a body-self which is essential for the development of identity.

We need to remember that the body is a primary means of learning and much of our intuition has a physical association before it is articulated vocally and verbally. I shall describe later how physical stages can be recreated in therapeutic work with children, particularly when there has been an absence of physical parenting, or neglect, or inappropriate handling such as physical and sexual abuse.

Eddie absorbed in projective play – the Lego will soon be as big as he is!

The second stage is **Projection** where the child relates more to the external world beyond the body. Although the child may respond physically to various media, nevertheless there is a focus on toys and substances and objects that are separate from the child. We could say that the child has moved on from exploration through movement to the exploration of other things. During the Projective stage children explore their own relationship to other objects as well as garnering them together in different types of relationships; things form patterns and shapes and represent things for the child and we see ever increasing use of symbols. Events and stories are dramatised through toys rather than the child taking on the roles themselves.

Children respond to the ritualisation of the same story being repeated as well as to the stimulus of a new story.

The third stage is that of **Role** where dramatic playing is seen most clearly and the child takes on various roles rather than projecting them through various toys and objects.

Through playing, the child is beginning to distinguish between everyday or mundane reality and playing or dramatic reality. Children begin to take examples of behaviour from adults, what is referred to as the 'process of role modelling'. These roles can often be rejected as the child approaches teen time, but again they can be rediscovered when adulthood is reached. There seems to be a closeness and a distance in relation to our peers and our parents which are ritualised dramatically through statements of sameness and difference. Adolescents like to dress up like their peers and very differently from their parents. Most young people loathe it when their parents dress too young!

Early Ritualised Patterns

Repetition and ritual establishes security and a knowledge base, for example:

- Mothers and babies create ritualised dramatic interactions as they rock and sing and make sounds together
- Babies create their own sound and movement patterns which are repeated and enjoyed
- Infants enjoy a mixture of the same and the new, that is, the ritual and the risk.

However, we must remember that the birth itself is ritualised through decisions regarding: hospital/home, birth-pool/bed, music/human instructions, 'nature'/drugs etc. The cutting of the cord and the inspection and disposal of the placenta all have ritualistic associations depending on class and culture. The cutting of the cord is also a symbolic expression used when children and adults take an independent step away from a family, a home, a long-term job and so on. When a baby is born there are celebrations, gifts, cards, 'wetting the baby's head', all part of the rite of passage and change of status of childbirth. The woman enters her new status of mother if it is the first child and the child is now *in vivo* instead of *in utero*. Celebrations express the relief at safe passage both at a literal as well as symbolic level.

There may then be the ritualisation of naming – what name? whose name? how many names? – culminating in official registration and possibly a naming ceremony. There are several stages that are ritualised through repetition, telling to others and recorded in a book: first sound, first word, first steps. All these progressions affirm the growing identity and independence of the child.

Young children play in dramatic form before they take on the adult convention of one person playing one character. They will often be narrator, director and various characters in quick succession and the drama is created *in situ*. It is usually improvised in the here and now but, even so, has its own beginning, middle and end. Dramatic playing demonstrates how quickly children are socialised into the idea of a structure where there has to be some kind of resolution.

The developmental paradigm of Embodiment–Projection–Role (EPR) is a broad categorisation to map the child's development from 0 to 5 years. There are many sub-stages and overlaps in between but they give a general framework within which play and playtherapy can be developed. EPR is appropriate as a working form for all groups of children because it is based on the general stages that all children appear to go through.

The Playtherapy Exercises through EPR

The following examples illustrate the EPR application in relation to specific creative material on the themes of rosebushes and monsters.

If we take Oaklander's rosebush exercise where a child is asked to imagine that she is a rosebush we might ask the child to physicalise the rosebush, to show how the rosebush grows, or move how it moves, to physically create the thorns, the flowers and so on. This would be an 'Embodiment' use of the rosebush where the child's body is the means of expression and the child may well be able to express not only gross body movement through the whole body but fine-tuned movement through body parts. It may be that her rosebush is not growing and that the flowers haven't grown or that somebody has stolen the flower. The rosebush in winter looks very different from the rosebush in the summer.

However if we asked the child to draw the rosebush, or to model it from clay, this would be 'Projection' where the child is using a medium outside the body or as an extension of the body to create the image. If the child is invited to become the rosebush, that is, to dramatise the character of the rosebush, which may well involve some movement as well as sound and possibly words, then we are using the 'Role' stage.

Whether we use the rosebush through Embodiment, Projection or Role or maybe, over time, all three, we will also invite the child to create the **story** of the rosebush. This story can be expressed physically through 'Embodiment' or written or told in 'Projection', or dramatised through 'Role'.

To give another example: if there seems to be an important theme of monsters, again monsters can be developed in any or all three of the stages. Thus the child can physicalise the monster – 'Embodiment', or draw, paint or model the monster – 'Projection' – or dramatise the monster – 'Role'. Again the monster will have a story to tell which can be physicalised, told or enacted.

The Fundamental Importance of EPR

The children with whom we work may show an automatic preference for working in a particular mode, especially when it is a choice between Embodiment and Projection. Children who have had very disturbing bodily experiences, and for whom touch is not a trusting experience, are more likely to feel comfortable with Projective work. By contrast, the child who has been ridiculed for their paintings and drawings, or has had their attempts to write stories ripped up and binned, may well be tentative about Projective work. Generally speaking, the child will dramatise and enact in a more fulsome way if they have had a firm grounding in Embodiment and Projection. (I am not using the word 'fulsome' here in a conventional sense, because I see it as having only positive connotations.)

Why are these three stages so crucial? Quite apart from the fact that they are the observed stages that we all pass through, there are certain intrinsic learnings that happen in these stages for life preparation.

I have already mentioned that during Embodiment we start to develop our body-self, but it is much more than this. We are learning an awareness of our own body as well as an awareness of the space surrounding it. Our body exists in space and is not lost in it. Furthermore, even though it may seem in adult life that our senses are being blunted with over-loaded music, fast food and over-stimulus of shape and colour, nevertheless differentiation of the senses is important in our relationship to others and the world. During the first year of life so much of our playing is sensory in terms of hearing, seeing, smelling, touching and tasting. We can observe how small babies differentiate sensory experience very quickly. Very small children will reject food because of its texture or its colour, or will be soothed by one set of rhythmic sounds rather than another. Sensory experience validates the child's relationship with the environment and initiates a whole range of choices in terms of soothing and stimulus, likes and dislikes.

Ultimately the child who develops a confident body-self will also be able to take reasonable physical risks. Indeed there are many children who have to be watched carefully because they take unreasonable physical risks. I have observed this in particular between the first and second year, when a child has become mobile and then wants to conquer the world. In the confident child there is a certain physical fearlessness that can cause great anxiety to parents and carers alike. However, the following observation of a physicalised rosebush story shows how many children do not acquire this confidence and ability to take risks.

> Sarah was six when she was referred to playtherapy. Her school had become increasingly concerned at her lone behaviour. Her fingernails were severely bitten and she would also bite the back of her hand until it bruised. She had also started pulling out her own hair strand by strand. She did as she was told but did not 'respond' when teachers asked for ideas or when children had to make choices in music and movement. Her drawings were safe and stereotyped. When she arrived at the playtherapy room she looked in awe at the choices of material but neither talked nor interacted with anything in the room. We sat in a quiet corner while I explained what could happen in the room and what I did. Initially we did some very simple repetitive action games to music. I call this 'ritualised movement'; it is repetitive and establishes safety. We led into the theme of trees through 'I had a little Nut Tree' and gardening through 'Mary, Mary'. We went from small actions to the song, to slightly bigger actions of things growing in the garden, except that her plants did not grow. Her response to the rosebush was to sit down in a foetal position and not move. When I introduced some elements, such as the sun or the wind, her response was to shrink even smaller. I verbally concluded the story by suggesting that this rosebush was waiting to grow but at the moment was resting in a safe place.

During the Projective stage we can see that various media become less part of the child's body and more part of the child's world. Toys, substances and objects are being organised outside the child's self and are symbolised to create situations. Whereas in the Embodiment stage the child explored the body and immediate bodily world, the child now extends into sensory play through a variety of materials. Initially it seems to be an exploration and a sensory stimulus rather than the actual 'making of something'. As the child gradually exercises control, patterns, shapes and groupings occur. Manipulative dexterity and eye/hand co-ordination increase and there is a sense of satisfaction from balancing something or the creation of a pattern. As a child develops the capacity to pretend, we observe an increase in symbolic playing with objects. Animals take on human characteristics, a box becomes a house, as a child is both creating and recreating past, present and future experiences as well as exploring the borders of the material itself. It is possible for the child to create an experience that is satisfying, or to recreate a pleasurable or frightening experience or to reformulate the experience in new ways that demonstrate the possibility of change. It would seem that children need to experience **sensory**, **exploratory** and **manipulative** play in order to be able to play objectively in symbolic form.

Symbolic play can only happen with the increasing development of the imagination

Projective play is important for learning how we organise the world outside and also to be able to have imaginative responses to the world of flexibility and change. It is a crucial period of child development where we can observe very clear phases of the progression from the sensory to the symbolic. This stage culminates in drawing and painting, story-telling and the creating of dramatic scenes through objects.

> When Sarah was invited to draw the rosebush out of a wide variety of colours she chose black and drew a minute bush shape in the corner of a piece of paper. Even the A4 piece of paper seemed too scary a space. She was able to say that the rosebush was hi ding. When I asked her who or what it was hiding from, she thought a moment and said 'the giant with the knives'. When I asked her what would make the rosebush feel safe, she said that it only felt safe when it was hidden.

We can observe elements of the Role stage very early in a child's development, even during the Embodiment stage, for example when they mimic their mother's facial expressions or echo her sounds. During the Projective stage, the child will dramatise scenes with objects and use different voices. This all culminates in the Role stage *per se* when the child takes on roles and characters and enacts scenes in dramatic form. By four to five years old the child takes on more and more roles and plays them in increasingly complex environments. The play world of the child has become more and more dramatised in form and content and the outcome is important. The child's vocal and physical range is expanded and dramas consist of both everyday situations and imagined events. I regard the importance of dramatic playing, and the dramatic processes, as so fundamental for human development that I shall write an extended chapter on that very topic.

> In my continued work with Sarah, it was obvious that the Role stage would not be appropriate and I made a decision to continue Projective work with her until she felt more secure. Once she was able to put the rosebush in a safe garden, to which she had the key, we went back to the Embodiment stage and physicalised this image. We actually built the safe garden in the play space. The transition into Role work came when Sarah felt ready to become the frightening things that were terrorising the rosebush. There were two figures who were outside the garden fence, the giant with the knives who was going to cut the rosebush and a fat woman who laughed. When Sarah said that she needed a white jacket to play the giant, my guess was that this was related to the time she'd had in hospital. Indeed the fat woman who laughed was a nurse who thought she could cheer Sarah up by laughing. Sarah, however, found this very frightening. The dramatisation in symbolic form of the tall and the fat giants and the scared rosebush culminated in Sarah being able to grasp her perception of the situation. I introduced the reality that although she had been very scared, she had in fact recovered. We used a lot of Embodiment work and Projective work to recreate these scary situations and slowly it took on the reality of 'the hospital' itself. By the end of her sessions, Sarah was able to draw a rosebush with flowers on it and her mother reported that the follow-up visit to the hospital had passed without major incident.

I have described in more detail the crucial importance of Embodiment – Projection – Role in ordinary healthy development and therefore as a methodology for doing playtherapy. I have illustrated Sarah's responses to the rosebush story in Embodiment, Projection and Role.

Let us now consider the theme of monsters in EPR and end with a story which encompasses all the three stages. It is important to remember that when a child embodies the subject of a frightening nightmare or event, they are already beginning to conquer that fear. In my own experience, rather than maintaining that children themselves are monstrous, I have noted that a recurring theme for them is that they are being devoured or attacked by monsters. Sometimes these are imaginary monsters and sometimes actual people or events are personified through monsters. Children will play at being monsters at all stages of play, like the child who crept up behind the sofa and said 'OOOH' to me and then said, 'Are you frightened?'

Monsters, however, take on many shapes and colours and sizes and the anxious child may have a very specific idea, as with Sarah's giant, of what the monster is like. Monster toys in the play space, such as dinosaurs and science fictions toys often create a bridge in monster play. By embodying the monster, that is, the actual physicalisation of a monster, the child already is diminishing its fearful aspects. Children will often respond to simple Embodiment exercises of being a monster and capturing a victim. The Embodiment is often accompanied by the frightening noises and sounds, the idea of claws and teeth and the idea of it being bigger than the child. There is also the opposite of this where a child or adult is actually frightened that they are monstrous and their actions may get out of control. I was reminded of this in work with an adult murderer, who created a lion mask out of fur fabric and said: 'I am Lion. People are very scared of me. I am a very lonely lion'.

Perhaps we need to remind ourselves that some children don't have a fear of monsters but have a fear of being a monster. This is after a response to abusive events that have made the child so angry, that the feelings are bigger than the child. This occurs especially when a child is unable to express these feelings – either they do not have the pathways of expression or else feelings have been forbidden. Frustrated parents, too, can imbue a child with a sense of monstrousness. The child can become the focus of all the anxieties of the parents' dream of life.

In Projective work on the theme of monsters we are able to get a clearer idea of the child's monster image. By expressing it on paper the monster is both given form and shape and, most important, it is contained by the borders of the paper. The Projected picture may well lead into Embodied work or Role work.

The stories that children have read or heard about monsters can become involved with their own fears, so an actual story also becomes the personal story of the child. Indeed the stories from a child's story book may well be a way in to accessing the child's monster fears.

In dramatic play which develops from the Role stage, monsters can be put in the context of a story which can be enacted in scenes. Monsters always 'do' something, whether it is chasing, or eating, or attacking, or wounding. Many myths and fairy tales from the ancient past to the present have a main theme of overcoming the monster. The slaying of Medusa, St George and the Dragon, the Three Billy Goats Gruff all entail the overcoming of the danger either by heroic deeds or by tricking the monster. I shall elaborate in a new publication the importance of developing both 'the hero' role and the

'Five-legged monster' by Harry, aged 4

Monster picture by Barney, aged 5

'The monster family' by Sophie, aged 8

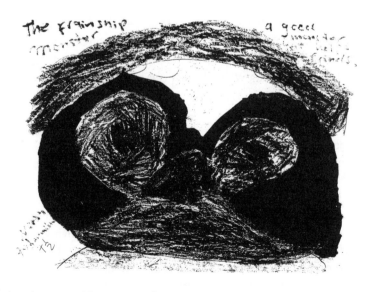

'The frainship monster' by Noam, aged 7

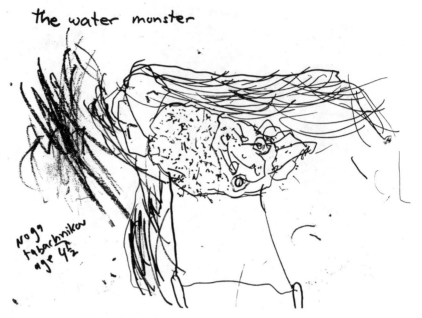

'The water monster' by Noga, aged 4

'trickster' role (Jennings 2000, in press). Tricksters are often neglected in our dramatic play and yet it is the trickster who usually outwits the bad character. The following story based on a North American Indian tale lends itself to dramatisation and improvisation and encompasses Embodiment, Projection and Role within a safe framework of successful outcome. Although the original story is about a young boy, it can be adapted as you see fit.

The Oseo Story

Once upon a time there was a little Indian boy who lived in a village near a large forest. His name was Oseo and he was always getting into scrapes and had lots of adventures. Winter had passed and the leaves were beginning to go on the trees and the birds were nesting in the forest and everything had a smell of newness and excitement. Oseo felt bored and as he sat outside his wigwam carving a piece of wood with his own knife, he decided to go into the forest, although he had been told never to go there on his own. He put on his jacket which had several pockets and crept quickly and quietly out of the village and climbed over the fence and went into the forest. Oseo remembered the forest code that he must 'stop, look and listen' whenever he heard a noise, in case it was something dangerous. As he went down the path into the forest humming to himself, he heard a rustle in the undergrowth so he stopped, looked and listened, and it was the green snake slithering away through the grass. The path got narrower and at some times he couldn't even see it and there were big creepers and branches blocking his way. He was climbing over logs and round bushes and sometimes had to cut his way through with his knife. Soon he came to a clearing and was quite tired from all the physical activity, so he sat down for a rest under a large tree. He saw a bird's egg at the foot of the tree and looked up and saw a bird's nest from which it had fallen. He picked it up very gently, stretched on tiptoe and put it back into the nest.

He was just deciding to go when the bird came to the edge of the nest and said, 'Oseo, I've got a present for you' and he stretched up his hand wondering what it could be. The bird put a dried pea into his hand and said, 'Don't lose it. It's magic'. So he put it in one of his pockets and continued on his way.

He found the path again but had to jump across several ditches and climb under branches and he heard a screeching sound so he stopped, looked and listened and saw the beautiful bird with the golden tail flying up to the treetops. He came to the bank of a river and was wondering if he could get across and saw a squirrel crying. The squirrel said that he wanted to cross the river but couldn't swim, so Oseo said, 'Don't worry. You sit on my head and I will take you across'. He slowly began to wade into the water; it was very cold and when his feet couldn't feel the bottom he began to swim very slowly in order to keep the squirrel safe. He got to the other side, put the squirrel down, and tried to dry his clothes. The squirrel was not to be seen, but it came back shortly and said, 'Oseo, I want to give you a present. You've been so kind to me'. The squirrel put an acorn in his hand and said, 'Don't lose it. It might help you one day. It's magic'.

Oseo climbed up a grassy bank and climbed over a fence into a very large field. He ran around trying to get dry when he suddenly heard an enormous noise and he stopped, looked and listened. Coming towards him was a huge giant making giant noises and as Oseo tried to run away, the giant shouted, 'I'm going to catch you, Oseo, and eat you'. The giant threw a net over Oseo and as he struggled and struggled the net got tighter and tighter so that he couldn't move at all. The giant said he was going to fetch a cooking pot. Oseo started to cry and thought he would never be able to go home again and suddenly he remembered his presents. He managed to get a hand free and got the magic pea, put it in his mouth, closed his eyes and wished very hard. Incredibly he began to get smaller and went on shrinking until he could climb out through one of the holes in the net. He began to run towards the river as fast as his little legs could carry him and the grass was like a forest and kept scratching his legs. Small stones now seemed like great rocks that he had to climb over. He could hear the giant roaring in the distance. He got to the fence and wriggled underneath it and roled head over heels down to the river bank and then realised he was too small to swim across. The giant was getting nearer. What could he do? He remembered his other present, the acorn, and put it in his mouth closed his eyes, and wished so very hard. It was working. He grew bigger and bigger until he was his normal size again. He raced into t he river and swam across as quickly as he could and didn't look behind him as he dashed into the forest. He had to jump across the ditches again, race across the clearing waving to the bird as he went and found the track that he had cut through the undergrowth. At last he got to the fence, climbed it quickly and quietly and went back to his wigwam with a big sigh of relief. He took off his wet clothes and wrapped himself up in his Indian blanket and started thinking about his big adventure as he went on carving his piece of wood. When his friends came past the wigwam they didn't even know he'd been out of the village.

The dramatisation of this story provides a multi-layered experience for the individual child or group. There is basic social learning in terms of what happens when rules are broken and the desirability of helping other creatures. However the story encompasses many other facets and integrates them into the one structure.

- The story starts and finishes in a safe place, the wigwam in the village
- There is a ritulisation of a control factor, that is, 'stop, look and listen'
- A range of physical movement is needed as well as physical control
- There are hostile elements in the forest to be overcome in a physical way
- The trickster elements enable the child to outwit the giant
- The hero elements demonstrate the child's capacity to care for the bird and squirrel
- The child is also helped by others
- The giant is the larger than life monster who is outwitted

- There is a resolution of the frightening episode even though the scary giant still exists.

We can see that the story of Oseo gives the opportunity for extended physicalised work, that is, Embodiment as the child battles through the forest, stretches, jumps, swims and so on, as well as shrinking and growing. There is Projective work too as Oseo sits and carves his piece of wood. Of course the overall structure is a dramatic one with Oseo playing the role of the hero/trickster and interacting with other roles: the bird, the squirrel and the giant. In this structure he doesn't become the giant, but finds a way to trick the giant through the help of others. There is an element of symbolic surprise for him when the mundane pea and acorn actually take on magical properties to help him rescue the situation.

There are many, many stories which contain these elements and which integrate a child's experience at many levels that can be used both for learning, re-learning and playtherapy intervention.

> Furthermore, not only can we observe the stages of developmental drama in babies and children, we can also see their increasing aesthetic sense, the pull for what feels 'right' in dramatic constructions and structures. The aesthetic pull interacts with the social expectations of roles and rituals in any given society. Thus from pre-birth and throughout life an individual is both dramatised and ritualised within a social milieu. But these forms need replenishing and sustaining. Dramatic and playful stru ctures are not something that we 'grow out of' with maturation; this view misconstrues the nature of drama and play. Drama and play are unique in their capacity to enable people to transform, transpose and reconstrue their lives continuously. (Jennings 1996, p.207)

George aged two-and-a-half demonstrated a capacity to understand his own size in relation to an ant when he came indoors and reported that he had caught an ant; 'but then I let it go again' he said. When asked why, he said 'I'm much bigger than the ant and it's frightened of me'.

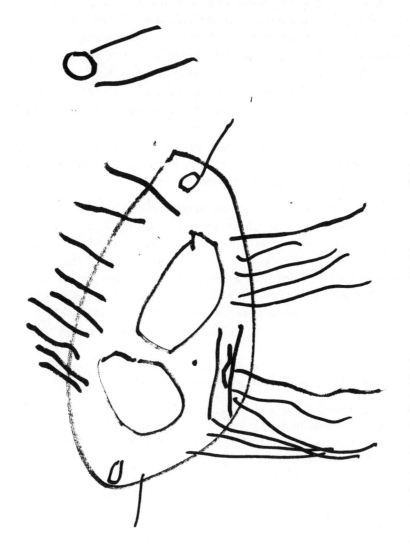

'The cross monster who has lost his rat. All the blood is running out of him' by George aged 3½

CHAPTER 4

Dramatic Play as a Basis for Living

Fool: That such a kind should play bo-peep.

(King Lear, I, iv, 174*)*

The three stages of Embodiment, Projection and Role outlined in the previous chapter are the basis of a dramatic world view. We actually construe the world in dramatic form and both experience and perceive it as a series of scenarios that we either observe as audience or play a part in as actor. We even dream in dramatic form and our thoughts and feelings are marshalled in dramatic episodes in our imagination. Time and again I have said that drama and, indeed, theatre, are a basis for living and the means through which we differentiate our everyday world from our imagined world, or in other words, everyday reality from dramatic reality.

We enact the drama of our lives through a series of tested roles and dramatic scenarios and the basis of these has been laid out in our early play experience and refined through childhood and adolescence. To achieve this we not only need the time and space to play but also a range of role models in our family and social environment with whom we can identify. It is through our roles that we are able to manage our lives satisfactorily and also to deal with unexpected events. If we have a flexible capacity for role play, it helps us to understand ourselves and others. Indeed we can say that role playing mediates between ourselves and others and is therefore the means whereby we develop both individual and social identity. Within the drama, the more we play a character who is not us, the more we learn about ourselves.

Robert Landy (1993) has written extensively about the theory and application of his role method and his Taxonomy of Roles is a useful method for assessment and therapeutic treatment. Landy suggests that when Hamlet says 'To be or not to be' it is usually said by actors as a statement rather than a question, even though the next phrase is – 'That is the question'. He says that

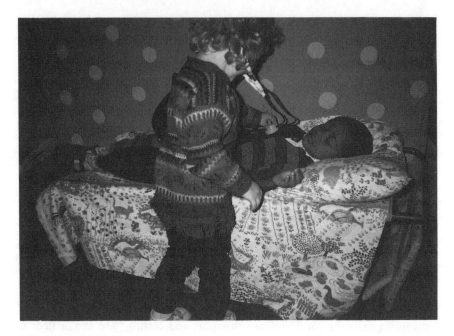

I'm the doctor – where does it hurt?

by allowing the sentence to be a question, as Shakespeare wrote it, we can understand the basic human dilemma: both to be and not be. He elaborates this concept in relation to the capacity of human beings to be both 'in role' and 'out of role' at one and the same time. I play a role and can observe myself playing that role, both on stage and in everyday life. If an actor is totally in role, then the borders and limits in relation to other people and the environment can be disrupted.

A recent example of this occurred in Israel where the actor playing Othello attempted to strangle Desdemona for real and she had to be hospitalised. Somebody suggested to me that a redeeming factor was that he was at least 'a hundred per cent acting'. My contention is that he wasn't acting at all, but merely being a murderous aspect of himself. Furthermore the idea that one can act 100 per cent is a contradiction in terms. The role or character should never take over completely. The same is true of everyday life – if my performance of a role is played out without the dimension that enables me to observe myself playing the role, then the role has taken over.

There is danger if the role has become me rather than being a part of me

I mentioned earlier that the foundations of drama and theatre are laid during pregnancy, when pregnant women role-reverse with their unborn child. The capacity to play 'as if' is an essential component of our dramatic development and without it we are mere creatures of impulse or can lapse into psychiatric disorder.

For many years I thought that the 'dramatic experience' started shortly after an infant was born. Dramatic 'engagement' was stimulated and reinforced during the first year of life. With my recent observations of pregnant women and babies I have revised this view; I now realise that the first dramatic interaction is usually set up between pregnant women and their unborn children. As I mentioned earlier:

> A woman talks to the imagined child, sings to it, asks it questions, and then she answers herself AS IF she is the child. It is such a simple everyday occurrence that I had not even noticed it. You may challenge my notion that this is a dramatic interaction. However, if you observe pregnant women talking in this way you will see that they are 'in role', using a different voice from their everyday communication; they reverse roles with the imagined child, as they answer themselves. (Jennings 1998, p.50)

'In role' as both mother and infant, the communication is often accompanied by movement and gesture such as rocking, stroking, patting and finger play; and the gestures change depending on who is speaking. A dialogue takes place with the mother taking both roles, using a dramatic convention of change in voice and movement in an imagined context, usually in a space set apart.

From birth, the dramatic imagination is developed through the stages of Embodiment, Projection and Role, so that by the time a child is five they are able to play in dramatic form. This is the bedrock of their emergent socialised and civilised behaviour.

As we are increasingly able to play 'as if' we are increasingly able to understand how the other person thinks and feels. This forms the basis for the development of empathy and even more important, the beginnings of our conscience. Conscience is the development of our sense of what is right and wrong and our moral stance in the world. It is that aspect of ourselves that can be troubled through careless actions or that regulates our potential for violent or anti-social behaviour.

If as children we do not experience the feelings of 'the other' and how it is **to be** them, and instead receive a moral code **from** others, we are more likely to grow up with a 'fear response' to the world rather than a deeper understanding of the way to live our lives, or the capacity to experience how other people feel. We learn through 'being the other' rather than receiving a moral code 'from the other'. Through playing we are able to discover our choices concerning the way to live and love. Playing has introduced us to a spiritual awareness.

One popular view is that actors don't have a conscience, and perhaps if we believed Jiminey Cricket in *Pinnochio*: 'what does an actor want with a conscience anyway', or the tabloid newspapers, then the Othello example would be justified. Actors after all were once amongst the rogues and vagabonds, and are still considered the same at least by insurance companies.

Artists and arts therapists, however, must have smiled wryly at a recent report from the Chief Medical Officer who, among a group of experts, has drawn up a plan 'to bring the arts from the margins to the centre of health care planning and practice, to harness the arts to reduce depression and combat social exclusion' (discussed on a radio programme).

The article goes on to discuss that artistic therapists can be used in community development and that the artistic approach to care can complement scientific and technological models that have been the driving force of treatment for most of this century.

However well-intentioned are these aims, it will take a long time to change popular opinion: play is generally more accepted than drama, especially for young children. Drama does not even rate highly on the school curriculum compared with music and art. Drama is still considered as something dangerous, questionable, unproved and at least a non-essential which can be dispersed with when cut-backs are needed. We still find the 'empty vessel' approach to child rearing, where children are supposed to be imbued with knowledge.

This is superbly described by Thomas Gradgrind in the following scene, where the schoolmaster Mr M'Choakumchild is being told how to approach his first day of instruction. Dickens' detailed description of Gradgrind displays such imagery that we are able to picture this awful gathering of what he later refers to as 'Murdering the Innocents'.

> 'Now, what I want is, Facts. Teach these boys and girls nothing but Facts. Facts alone are wanted in life. Plant nothing else, and root out everything else. You can only form the minds of reasoning animals upon Facts: nothing else will ever be of any service to them. This is the principle on which I bring up my own children, and this is the principle on which I bring up these children. Stick to Facts, Sir!'

The scene was a plain, bare, monotonous vault of a schoolroom, and the speaker's square fore-finger emphasised his observations by underscoring every sentence with a line on the schoolmaster's sleeve. The emphasis was helped by the speaker's square wall of a forehead, which had his eyebrows for its base, while his eyes found commodious cellarage in two dark caves, overshadowed by the wall. The emphasis was helped by the speaker's mouth, which was wide, thin, and hard set. The emphasis was helped by the speaker's voice, which was inflexible, dry, and dictatorial. The emphasis was helped by the speaker's hair, which bristled on the skirts of his bald head, a plantation of firs to keep the wind from its shining surface, all covered with knobs, like the crust of a plum pie, as if the head had scarcely warehouse-room for the hard facts stored inside. The speaker's obstinate carriage, square coat, square legs, square shoulders, – nay, his very neckcloth, trained to take him by the throat with an unaccommodating grasp, like a stubborn fact, as it was, – all helped the emphasis.

'In this life, we want nothing but Facts, Sir; nothing but Facts!'

The speaker, and the schoolmaster, and the third grown person present, all backed a little, and swept with their eyes the inclined plane of little vessels then and there arranged in order, ready to have imperial gallons of facts poured into them until they were full to the brim. (*Hard Times*, p.182)

Children are still treated with over-control and cruelty, and Alice Miller (1983) suggests that it is a continuation of the way we attempt to destroy the child in ourselves:

The scorn and abuse directed at the helpless child as well as the suppression of vitality, creativity, and feeling in the child and in oneself permeate so many areas of our life that we hardly notice it anymore. Almost everywhere we find the effort, marked by varying degrees of intensity and by the use of various coercive measures, to rid ourselves as quickly as possible of the child within us – i.e. the weak, helpless, dependent creature – in order to become an independent, competent adult deserving of respect. When we re-encounter this creature in our children, we persecute it with the same measures once used on ourselves. And this is what we are accustomed to call 'child-rearing'. (p.58)

EPR leading to dramatic play is probably one of the few ways in which we can redress the damage. Dramatic play is where the three stages are integrated and is the stepping-stone to drama itself.

Dramatic play, which progresses from Role, is a stage in normal development and may be applied in playtherapy. It develops a sense of 'self and other' through appropriate role modelling, a child develops both a sense of autonomy as well as a sense of belonging to the group. The development of understanding, on the one hand, and increased knowledge of 'self and other', on the other, grow in tandem as a child has the opportunity to be in and out of roles. However, it is important that the child is increasingly aware of the separation of the reality of the imagination from the reality of everyday, so that there is no fusion between these two modes of experience. One will feed the other; for example my experiences in drama will help me know more about my everyday world just as new knowledge acquired in my everyday world will imbue my drama with new riches. The child or adult who cannot eventually differentiate between ordinary life and imagined life, is likely to suffer serious emotional damage.

Batman

The bullet points below form a summary of the progression of role skills and role expansion as the child matures, from birth to six years.

- Imitation of sounds, gestures, reactions
- Innovation of new sounds, gestures, reactions
- Pretending to be adult, animal, monster
- Role-reversing with special toys
- Projective roles through objects
- Personifying family members or TV characters, with variation and not just replication
- Role-taking and the beginning of identification
- Enactment of roles and scenes with environments
- Dramatic play separated from other play activities
- Drama. All of the above and increased improvisation. Ideas are tested and repeated.

Throughout our dramatic development as simplified above, there is an increasing artistic and aesthetic awareness. Children develop a sense of it being 'right' and this is usually at a 'felt' level rather than being imposed by adults. Unfortunately, now that so many drama props are available ready-made, it takes away the projective process of making masks and costumes for the drama. Children can develop a sense that their own paper-bag mask is never as good as the one bought in the shop. However when I am running play and drama workshops, the **making** of the tools or props is an important part of the process of creating and dramatising with them.

Why is there still antipathy towards the idea of dramatic play, drama and theatre? I have heard clinicians say to me that they will do role play which has nothing to do with drama, or that they do enactment but it is not an artistic method. The word 'role' in fact originated in the theatre from the roll of paper on which an actor's part was written in the days when whole scripts would be too expensive to produce. Nowadays the word 'role' has come to mean the different sorts of behaviours that people learn in order to be fully socialised adults. My contention is that the only way that we can really learn these roles is within the context of dramatic play and drama.

The moment one takes on a role one is beginning to step into another reality and the main difference is the amount of distance between the role and the person involved, or the scene and the person's life experience. I firmly believe that by maximising the distance between the self and the character and the scene, paradoxically one comes closer to the self. Distancing enables us to see the 'wood for the trees' in a situation that might otherwise be too overwhelming or too complicated to comprehend. Contrary to the claims of conventional psychotherapy that there are internal experiences that need to be externalised, the uses of dramatic forms of therapy enable a constant feedback system between inner and outer experience. There is a constant expansion of self and the world through the artistic use of playtherapy rather than a reductionist minimalist view from a rigid framework, which can happen in some other therapies.

No discussion of the field of drama and play is complete without exploring the phenomenon of transitional material. Donald Winnicott (1974) first coined the phrase 'the transitional object' to describe the 'comfort blanket' or soft toy that the child fiercely possesses at around a year old. Winnicott suggests that it is the child's first symbol and represents the absent mother. It represents the transition between the child's relationship with its mother and the child being able to tolerate the mother's absence. In play therapeutic terms the transitional object forms the bridge between Embodiment and Projection in EPR development. If we examine it more closely it has an integrative function as it takes on all the properties of Embodiment, Projection and Role.

- The child strokes, smells and caresses the blanket or cloth – Embodiment

- The child invests it with several symbols as an object outside itself – Projection

- The child relates to it in dramatic form as the object is named and accompanies the child on adventures – Role.

The transitional object, as well as having these physical and projective qualities for the child, becomes the child's dominant other character. The child will talk to it and ask it questions and then answer on its behalf, that is, the child is able to 'role-reverse' just as the mother was able to 'role-reverse' symbolically with her unborn child. Most people can remember an early toy or piece of cloth or bedding that they felt very strongly about and that they had a unique relationship with. Many people keep their teddies and dolls and remember their names. Indeed I wonder if the current emphasis on teddy bear collecting fulfils a generalised need to reconnect with our transitional object.

Alan, nine, was referred for playtherapy after being described as tyrannical in his playing. The teachers reported that he was controlling other children, constantly interrupted her in her teaching, and his mother in particular was subject to continued criticism of anything she did at home. Alan's life needed to be ordered and precise and he spent long periods of time on his computer and in mathematical homework. The school also reported cruelty to animals which had been observed by other children, including pulling wings off moths and butterflies, jumping on frogs and unduly teasing local cats.

When Alan saw that he was going to see a female therapist he became quite belligerent and folded his arms and said he wasn't going to do anything and said that I must be stupid. He got a pocket computer game out of his pocket and started playing with it.

I must confess that I was completely fazed at this unprepossessing start and tried to remind myself that I must 'start where the child is at' and of course he was, in fact, playing, albeit in a technological and individual way. I tried to stimulate a dialogue about his computer game and he answered in monosyllables without looking up. I said to him that I knew lots of different ways of playing but I didn't know computer games and asked if he would be willing to show me. With a withering look and a big sigh he held the game out while he showed me what he did and, with a brainwave, I suggested to him that it was rather like my calculator. I took my calculator out and started to use it while he continued with his game. I asked him if he was willing to swop over and let me have a go and after a moment's thought he agreed, but he became very testy with me and told me I wasn't doing it properly, and I said, 'OK, you're brilliant at this, but maybe I'm brilliant at other things'. He said, 'Yes, but girls aren't good at anything'. So I suggested that we each wrote down a list of what we were good at (I could have used the Mandala Technique described in Chapter 9), and he listed computers, maths and so on, and I wrote down, being a little economical with the truth, drawing, painting and clay. I asked him if he felt good, being good at these things, and he shrugged and suddenly said, 'Are you scared of me?' I answered 'I'm not scared, but I'm puzzled about you. I don't really understand what you want to do'. And I said to him, 'Are you scared of me?' and he said 'Not likely', but turned away and went back to his game.

I took out a jigsaw puzzle of a farm with a tractor on it. Somehow it seemed important for me to do something connected with machinery and I started making the puzzle. After a few moments he turned to look at what I was doing and said, 'I'd like to drive one of those', pointing to the partly formed tractor. 'Where would you drive it?' I asked and he said, 'I'd like to work on a farm, but my dad says it's just for thickos'. As I finished the puzzle I said to him, 'Look, we could play at farms if you wanted to' and he said nothing, and then said, 'Maybe, but don't tell anybody'. It was the end of the session and I felt very confused about the best way forward.

In the intervening time I really wondered what on earth I might do next. I thought that using the small farm animals and people and buildings might be seen as babyish and so many of the stories about farms were in books for very young children. He was a highly intelligent boy, already very sophisticated on a computer, who had let drop that he would like to work on a farm. I obtained a couple of adult posters about farming and a pack from an international charity that talked about the growing and irrigation of crops with various pictures and even some seed samples. I had these in the room and decided just to see what would happen, which after all is the best way to approach any playtherapy, though I must confess I felt far from comfortable.

> Alan came into the room slightly less reluctantly than on his first visit, though not exactly with excitement. He came and sat at the play table and said to me, 'Do you want to have a go with this? It's too easy for me now'. He handed me another computer game that he'd outgrown and showed me how to use it, so for a little while we each of us played with our games and every so often I asked him for assistance.
>
> After ten minutes I asked if he had thought any more about the farm and he looked very wary. I said I had found some pictures, which I laid out on the table. It immediately captured his attention as he closely studied ways to sink a well and draw water and how to harvest and store grain. I asked him if this was anything like what he wanted to do when he drove a tractor, and he nodded. He said, 'I don't want to be a farmer that works with animals, but I want to grow things. I would like to be a farmer that grows crops and harvests them'.
>
> I suggested that we could plant the wheat grains that came in the pack and see them grow over the weeks and for the first time he smiled. Together we planted the seeds and wrote a label for them with the name and the date. He then said he would like to draw a tractor, which he did in meticulous detail and then he drew a shed round it and said that the tractor would never come out of its shed, that it would never be used, so I said that we could pretend that it can come out of the shed and see what

meticulous detail and then he drew a shed round it and said that the tractor would never come out of its shed, that it would never be used, so I said that we could pretend that it can come out of the shed and see what happens. So I brought one of the toy tractors onto the table and some bricks. Alan built a shed and put the tractor inside and said, 'This is a secret tractor that nobody knows about. It's not allowed to come out'. I said, 'If we pretend?' so he looked a little wary but said, 'OK, as long as nobody sees' and he tentatively brought the tractor out of the shed, pushed it around the table and then put it back again. I gave him back his computer game, but he asked if I would I keep it until next week and I agreed that I would look after it in my drawer and that perhaps we would continue the tractor story next week.

These two sessions really took me by surprise. I had never come across a tractor waiting to burst out of somebody, although I had encountered other sorts of people, or characters, or magical entities, but the locked-up secret tractor seemed crucial for Alan. In these two sessions I worked projectively with the computer game and with the tractor drawing, the toy and the bricks and it seemed that that would be the safe way to proceed.

One of the teachers at the school reported that he was a little less controlling. Subsequent sessions enabled us on the one hand to watch the wheat grow and on the other to elaborate the tractor story, and after a few weeks the tractor was able to come out for longer periods of time and function as a tractor.

It was time for a family conference and I and the team had a meeting with the parents. They said there had been a slight modification of his behaviour at home. I asked the parents to tell me a little bit more about themselves and the family and an extraordinary scenario emerged. Alan's mother had in fact been a farmer herself as part of a large farming family in rural Shropshire. She had met Alan's father at an agricultural fair when he was a young representative from a bank. The friendship blossomed and she left the farm and moved a long way away when her husband was transferred to a larger bank in a small city. His career in the bank had flourished and he revelled in the fact that he had a rural domesticated wife. She, in fact, was not flourishing and yearned for the open spaces and the chance to grow things. The communal gardens of their expensive town house did not meet these needs.

When Alan was born, his father was sure that he would grow up to be like himself and encouraged every aspect of his mathematical and computer interest. Alan of course was presented, it would seem, with a dilemma from his parents since the rural idyll, of which he had heard in stories from his mother, was a way of life that was denigrated by his father. Therefore the tractor had to remain secret, I thought to myself.

It was recommended that his mother and father should have some couple therapy parallel to Alan's work, and that there should be occasional sessions of family therapy. Fortunately for Alan, the playtherapy intervention had been early enough to bring about some profound positive change. He was able to embark on secondary school with an acceptance of the value of a more broadly based curriculum together with an agreement from his father that occasional school holidays could be spent on the grandparénts' farm.

This situation was a reminder to me not to jump to premature conclusions about the possible motivations for the therapy that was needed. The referral letter had so many classic symptoms in it that it would have been easy to go up an inappropriate cul-de-sac. The secret tractor remains for me an important symbol of the mysteriousness of playtherapy. There are people who have suggested that my intervention is educational rather than therapeutic. However, any starting point is the beginning of engagement in the playtherapy, and the planting of an actual garden with the grain seeds is just as legitimate as drawing a garden.

Through the tractor, Alan was able to make the transition into a projected dramatic scene which communicated the core of his dilemma.

Despite ambivalence about the word 'drama', dramatic action and representation underpin most of our waking and sleeping life. We play roles, enact scenes and imagine in dramatic form how things might be or how they were. Our imagination is dramatic in form and content whether we are awake or asleep.

> The more we are exposed to theatre art, the more skilled we become in being able to communicate in dramatic form about our experiences. I have observed a tendency in dramatherapy groups for participants to rush into an improvisation and complete it very quickly. They are often reluctant to stay with the artistic process. Then they are amazed where the journey takes them if they continue. Repetition of art takes us into greater depth. I suggest that from birth we are able to respond dramatically to the world around us, and that during the early years we are both player and playwright in the way we start to construe our perception of the world. If this aspect of ourselves is allowed to develop we become more adept at dramatic construction and it is enhanced and

enlarged by our increasing imagination. Our imagination is essentially dramatic in nature as we remember and recount not necessarily events that are 'dramatic' in themselves but rather, we dramatise them as a way of communicating them. Placing them in dramatic form means that they are manageable and containable and that we can communicate the events to others. (Jennings 1998, p.35)

If I am able to play out a situation I can understand it more, and if it is played out through dramatic distance, I am likely to understand it better.

If there are adults who provide role models for me rather than only telling me what to do, then I can learn appropriate role behaviour.

If I can work collaborating with others in dramatic play or drama then I am becoming socially skilled at co-operation and team-work.

Dickens refers to imagination as 'fancy' and throughout his life maintained in his thinking the idea that people 'instructionally' respond imaginatively to the world around them. He sees 'fancy' as something belonging to children and their sense of wonder and curiosity:

It was an attribute especially prominent in children – Sissy's untutored responses to questions in the schoolroom show more wisdom than the combined learning of adults there present – and it was intimate with an inclination to respond sympathetically to the feelings of others. Fancy, Dickens insisted, was not an acquired taste, but an inalienable part of being human. For the hands, it offers relief from the grinding drudgery of their existence; for Louisa, it represents possibilities of fulfilment not catered for in her father's system. Spontaneity, freedom, release, enjoyment, fellow-feeling, contentment with one's lot – these were the values which Dickens associated with fancy, and these were the values which he held up as positive alternatives to the leaden Philosophy of Fact.

And this is where the circus comes in. With its horses, riders, acrobats, and clowns, the circus existed precisely as a stimulus to the vital power of fancy. Exotic costumes and skilful tricks, exuberant energy and glittering spectacle provided pleasures which were decidedly non-Utilitarian; instead, they offered an escape from the hardships and cares of daily life, and an escape into a fantasy world of glamour, excitement, and novelty. Performing to an audience, it offered shared pleasures, with no pretence of instruction or utility, but with the simple and humble purpose of providing amusement. This function is explicitly spelled out by the circus proprietor in *Hard Times*, Mr Sleary, when he tells Mr Gradgrind, 'people must be amuthed, Thquire, thomehow ...they can't be alwayth a working, nor yet they can't be alwayth a learning. Make the betht of uth; not the wurtht'. (Schlicke, 'Introduction to *Hard Times*', in Dickens 1989, p.xviii)

Hard Times not only documents attitudes towards children, it also delightfully shows us how circus people, strolling 'players' like actors, show an integrity and a dedication and a loyalty to each other. All these qualities can be developed from dramatic play.

Mother: George, you're a real little terror aren't you?

George (aged 3): No, I'm not! I'm a terranasaurus.

Harry's Tractor

CHAPTER 5

Practical Playtherapy: Embodiment

Bottom: Let not him that plays the lion pare his nails.

(A Midsummer Night's Dream, IV, ii, 41*)*

As part of Embodiment we need to look at how we can build a repertoire of healthy touching bearing in mind that many children have not experienced sufficient human contact or else have experienced touching in a destructive and damaging way. Touch must not be imposed on children because that in itself can constitute abuse. Children do not come to playtherapy to sit on the therapist's lap and be cuddled. As my colleague Ann Cattannach stated very firmly: 'Adults do not go to therapy to cuddle their therapist, so why should this be acceptable for children? Furthermore, too many classical therapists demand a dependency from their young clients which can be very traumatic when the therapy ends.' (Personal communication.)

Attachment may not mean touch. As I discussed earlier, many children come into therapy who have not for whatever reason formed a primary attachment to a parent or carer. It is even more dangerous to work with such children on a 'transference relationship', that is, where the therapist becomes a primary attachment figure. It is infinitely healthier to use what Cattanach describes as a 'narrative structure, where the transference takes place in the story and characters in the story, rather than on the therapist themselves' (personal communication).

O'Connor (1991), quoted in Cattanach (1994), explores the role of the therapist through his unconventional (i.e. not psychoanalytical) description of the transference which happens in the playtherapy process.

> O'Connor's concept of transference is broader. He regards transference not only as emotions, thoughts and behaviour which the client manifests within the context of the therapeutic relationship, but also as the treatment-related interaction between the child and therapist and the

child's ecosystem. That is, transference on the part of the child also occurs when she reacts to events in her ecosystem in a manner consistent with issues occurring in therapy.

In the same way, countertransference refers to the emotions, thoughts, and behaviours that the therapist brings to her interactions with the child's ecosystem, whether it is the child's carers, teachers, social worker, or anyone else. Most playtherapists have to be involved with the child's ecosystem, and this makes the clarity of boundaries difficult to maintain and very complex.

O'Connor says that the therapist should be alerted to three types of transference in which children commonly engage.

At some point in the process the child is likely to develop a parental transference. She may react towards the therapist as the 'good' parent or the 'bad' parent. If the therapy is going well, then the transference is likely to be the 'good' parent. It is important to help the child realise that this is a fantasy and will not become a reality. (The use of the story in 'Bye Bye Baby' as described in Chapter 2 shows an appropriate way of helping the child understand the role of the playtherapist).

A second common transference reaction is when the child perceives the therapist as all powerful and able to solve all the child's problems.

The third type of transference concerns the child taking emotions, thoughts, or behaviours out of the therapy space and into the ecosystem. For example, the child who becomes very dependent and clingy in therapy becomes so at home and the child, whose behaviour was already problematic, deteriorates as the therapy continues.

Therefore it is important that the therapist actively explains to the child and her carers the underlying needs of the child which stimulate these transferences. (Cattanach 1994, pp.57–8)

I personally feel very strongly with Cattanach that one advantage of playtherapy and dramatherapy, because of the very nature of the materials used, is that transferences and their resolution can take place within the material rather than with the therapist. In dramatherapy we see that transferences and similar phenomena are related to roles and characters where the clients themselves can also experience being the transferential figure. I often use masks to create a range of roles that clients invest with significant elements of their own lives. Similarly in playtherapy the same process can occur as the playtherapist co-creates a narrative journey with the child in a process from hurt to healing.

Touch and Texture

Just as a small infant explores the texture of a range of objects and substances, I find that a starting point in playtherapy can be a range of stuff with contrasting surfaces. Touch of 'things' can be a starting point for establishing trustful touching. One technique I use is what I describe as the **texture box**. The box itself can be textured on the outside, either carved or inlaid or covered in some type of fabric, thus providing a tactile experience before it is even opened. Inside the box is a selection of objects such as: velvet, sandpaper, egg shells, twigs, shells, sand, wool, fur fabric, play slime, jelly balls and stones. Children like the surprise of opening a box and seeing what's inside and the texture box is one of many containers that I use in order to create a story. As children pick up the different things, I encourage them to use words to describe them and to acknowledge the ones they like and the ones they don't like. As a child gets more confident they can do this exercise with their eyes closed, but initially it is important not to have any sudden negative surprises.

> Once upon a time the sun was shining and the sand and shells were on the beach. The water came in and brought lots of rough stones and scratchy things. The seagull flew away with the egg shell.

Similarly, playing with sand and water produces contrasting physical experiences, as does finger paint or play dough or modelling clay. The playtherapist needs to remember that there should be a range of textures, including some that can be controlled such as stones and twigs, and some that cannot be controlled such as water and wet sand.

Another useful technique is the **texture bag** which itself needs to be made of a textured material, perhaps canvas, velvet or hessian. Inside it there is a range of suitable objects such as: scrubbing brush, orange, marble, wooden spoon, pan scrubber, fossil, pencil, scrumpled paper... The child and the therapist take it in turns to take an object out of the bag, keeping their eyes closed. They have to describe it and then guess what it is. These objects will also have various associations and even a seemingly innocuous thing may have very unpleasant associations for a child. For example, a child who had been regularly spanked with a wooden spoon was very scared when discovering it in the bag. This led to a developed session which focused on the context of the unpleasant object, and we created different stories where wooden spoons had pleasant functions as well as unpleasant ones. We then made some wooden spoon dolls and created stories that were important to the child.

Texture boxes and bags are important in the playtherapist's repertoire, not only to develop touch but also as a stimulus to develop into other activities.

- The child rediscovers a range of touch that may be absent or distorted
- This will enable a greater range of expression and communication
- This will allow a greater accessibility to the child's life experience
- It acts like a loop system in which the child is able to access and transform his or her experience
- Therapeutic expression and the development of play ability are mutually enhancing and beneficial.

When to be Extra Cautious

The following are suggestions for dealing with the child who avoids any touch at all costs in the playtherapy. Some therapists believe that touch should not be a part of the therapy, that the therapist should be outside the physical orbit of the child, and that the media and toys are the means of contact taking place. The Playtherapy Method includes a range of physical techniques, many of which involve touch. Most children's play and games involve varying degrees of touch and I regard it as artificial not to allow this as part of the therapeutic value of the play. Obviously the therapist both exercises care in the choice of methods and is scrupulously honest about his or her personal motives. Many playtherapists now videotape their sessions in order to protect themselves should there at any stage be misunderstanding of their intervention.

However much we may feel that appropriate touching is healthy and therapeutic, there are some children who totally refuse to touch or to allow touch and who will always set up physical distance between themselves and the therapist. It is as if the child has drawn a large circle of personal space around his or her body and does not want this to be violated.

In these cases the playtherapist needs to experiment. It may mean in the early days that the child plays at a distance as long as the therapist does not get 'too close'. The therapist can bridge the space by continuing to talk to the child while at the same time respecting the space. Walkie-talkies and telephones are useful ways of bridging the distance vocally. Container play – as described in earlier chapters – allows symbolic safety and both child and therapist can play in containers. String, streamers and 'falls' (beautiful long strips of chiffon available from sari shops) can all serve to make contact, to form an attachment. It is an intermediary between adult and child – I do not think that this necessarily establishes a symbolic umbilical cord – but a symbolic attachment leads to contact and engagement.

The child who does not want to touch will sometimes show violence towards toys in the playtherapy environment. It is important to be clear with the child about ground rules here – and whether some things can be knocked about or not. It may be that a child is so terrified of his or her own potential violence that he or she will not allow the touch of other people. One little girl, for example, had been told repeatedly, 'You'll be the death of me' by her mother.

Sensory Play

Texture play is a part of a large range of methods under the heading of 'sensory play' which is important for children who have organic damage or whose senses have been dulled through early experience or neglect. All children have a potential sensory self through which they understand and process the world around them. An important part of playtherapy should involve all or some of the senses in playing or in games.

Tea parties with real or pretend food, washing and drying dolls, hide and seek, tiptoe games, for example, all involve the senses. Playtherapists may create their own sensory stories or use existing myths and fairy tales. The Oseo story, which is told in Chapter 3, is one example of a story that involves the senses.

I also use a **sensory box** which contains a variety of materials which again should be a box that is 'special', for example it can be carved or lined with velvet and contain sounds such as squeakers or whistles, smells such as a lavender bag or perfume sample, nuts and raisins or chocolate mints, a hologram or small toy, a hand cream sample or piece of silk. Sensory boxes can be explored for themselves or, again, can lead into play or story-making.

As always, the playtherapist needs to be vigilant if any of the sensory experience produces an adverse reaction. For example, whereas the use of hand cream can be a very self-soothing experience, on the other hand it can recall the unpleasant stickiness and mess of sexual abuse. Similarly, the pleasant perfume for some children of a lavender can also remind certain people of the thinly disguised smell of a dead body that has been doused in lavender water. A playtherapist must also be careful not to bombard a child with too much stimulus, which can be overwhelming and impede therapeutic development. Although sensory play is primarily Embodiment work, through stories, it can also lead into Projective and Role work.

Physical Play

Young children spend many of their waking hours in movement play, in sitting, crawling, climbing, rolling and pretending to fly. Movement play needs to be re-experienced with a damaged child who is often physically tense and apprehensive. During normal development a child moves from rolling over to sitting to crawling to standing and it is possible in imaginative ways to recreate these stages.

> Rolling is a series of falls, the safest the body can do, it involves letting go of weight and giving in to the pull of gravity. Tense, anxious children roll rigidly like a log, with their forearms protecting the chest and the head lifted. (Sherborne 1990, p.10)

When the child rolls unaided, he or she is managing their whole body in relation to the floor. The floor supports the child and the floor is something you cannot fall off. The child receives continuous feedback in relation to the temperature, texture and resilience of the floor. We must not forget that a baby's first whole body movement is to roll over. If the child is ready, the therapist can play at both rolling the child and being rolled by the child. In order to develop a co-operative endeavour we can *allow* ourselves to be rolled, that is, we are working *with* each other. By contrast, we can *resist* being rolled, that is, we are working *against* our partner. This is also important as the child is learning autonomy and the capacity to say 'no' through their own body. Rolling is very important for developing not only control and touch, but also the body-self.

All kinds of stories can be created where characters can roll down hills, such as logs or beach balls. Similarly the other physical stages such as sitting and crawling can be encompassed within a story. Some children may develop confidence through moving in different ways to rhythm and music. One colleague of mine working with an eight-year-old had to have a ritualised beginning and end to dancing to Spice Girls music.

Other Embodiment methods include:

- Free rolling into the centre of the room and out again
- Groups can roll over each other to develop trust and confidence

- Rolling in jelly, one person is floppy and the other person tries to roll them over
- Holding a partner by the ankles and giving them a ride
- One person lies on their side and their partner unfolds them and folds them up again
- One person lies in a star shape as if they are stuck to the floor and their partner has to unstick them
- Sitting back to back and giving a partner a ride by pushing against their back
- Similarly, resisting being pushed, which quite literally teaches a child 'not to be pushed around'
- Sitting in threes, one behind the other, and all trying to move together
- Letting this develop into a story of the sea and the three becoming a boat
- Sitting in pairs holding hands and a third person trying to get in
- Vary this with one person trying to get out
- Crawling under and over other people in the room
- Making a bridge for the child or children to crawl under
- For larger groups, making a tunnel for children to crawl through
- Letting one person lie across several people's backs and rocking them from side to side.

The above exercises have all been influenced by the work of Veronica Sherborne (1990) who makes the point that human bodies are the best climbing apparatus. The human body has many possibilities to be climbed, to be ridden, or to provide a shelter, a crane, and so on.

Playtherapists will find that children will enjoy certain aspects of ritualised repetitive movement and when they feel secure will enjoy elaborating and taking risks with the various movements. Physical play establishes a safe basis for the child from which other types of play can develop. The following stories were all elaborated out of basic movement work, that is, Embodiment.

Embodied Stories

The Log Story

> Once upon a time, there was a very thick forest. There were so many trees that they were crowding each other out, and all their branches were tangled together. (*Group stand very close together, intertwined*) The forester decided that some of the trees would have to be cut down and taken down the river. (*Half the group become logs and the other half roll them down the hill*) The logs are rolled down the hill and into the river where they float down to the farm. They float under bridges (*made by the group*), and at times they float so near each other that they get stuck. (*This guides proximity and distance of movement*) When the logs come to the farm, they are pulled out of the water and left to dry on the bank.

The simple log story above (which is ecologically sound and non-gender-specific) shows the following movement and social progression.

1. Whole group: body-mass – touching and intertwined

2. Whole group to pairs: body-pairing – logs and log-pushers

3. Pairs to individuals: body-individuation – floating down river.

4. Whole group: body-mass – at log jam

5. Group to individual: body-individuation-log jam freed

6. Individual to pair: body-pairing – logs and log-pullers

7. Pair to individual: body-individuation – logs drying.

This story can be taken further with transformation – from logs to shelters, for example, depending upon the stage of the group.

The Boat Story

> Once upon a time, some small boats were tied up in the harbour (*people in threes one behind the other*) resting and, very gently, rocking from side to side. They decided to go out to sea to look for adventure. They all set off out of the harbour. (*Groups move themselves across the floor*) The wind began to blow, the waves became stronger and the boats rocked from side to side. (*Groups sway, using larger movements*) A big wave and gust of wind came up and blew the boats over and everyone was swimming in the sea. (*Boats disintegrate and individuals start to swim*). All the people were huddled up in the sea, swimming around looking for their own boat. Gradually, the wind subsided and the waves got smaller and the people found their

own boat. (*Small groups find each other*) The boats decided that they had had a big adventure and went back to the harbour again. (*Boats in threes move across the room*) They arrived in the harbour, tied themselves up, and rested. (*People close eyes and lean and support each other*)

This story takes people from relaxation to stimulation and back again – from the known to the unknown. It uses the following movement and social progression:

1. Groups of three: touch and co-operation, bodies relaxed and still

2. Bodies working together to move out to sea

3. Bodies moving vigorously together

4. Small groups to individuals: bodies individuate, floating and swimming vigorously

5. Individuals to small groups: bodies relating, rediscovering threes

6. Small group relaxing and touching: bodies working together; return to harbour.

It represents a maturational step when children can progress from working with a partner to working in a threesome. If children are not able to make this maturational step, the three will break up into a pair and an individual (less often, to three individuals).

Again, the basic story above can be built on using the different elements of weather; light and dark; visiting the world under the water.

I have used a variation of the above story with a remedial infant class with learning and behavioural difficulties. We progressed from the boat into the sea and then created the world of the sea with everyone choosing what they wanted to be. People chose to be pieces of coral, fish of different sorts and sizes, crabs, floating seaweed.

I then asked each child to describe their shape and colour and to show how they moved. (The children had been stimulated by a recent TV educational programme about the seabed.) After we had explored under the sea, we swam to the surface, found our boats, and sailed back to land again.

At this point, the class teacher peered through the door and asked if she could see what they were doing. The children returned to the seabed again, resumed their previous roles, and described their colours, shapes and movements. They were greeted by the following response: 'Children, this is very silly. You saw that programme on a black-and-white television!' What does a hapless playtherapist do at this point?

On this particular occasion, I intervened and said: 'Let me explain. We were *imagining* what colours were under the sea. I'm developing the use of language at the moment.' Honour seemed to be satisfied for the teacher and the children stopped looking crestfallen.

The Magic Forest Story

Once upon a time, a group of small animals was travelling through the countryside. They came to a magic forest. (*Half the group act as forest as individual trees and half act as animals*) The animals came into the forest looking for a resting place. (*Encourage the 'trees' to stand legs apart and body bent*)

Each animal found a shelter and curled up inside (*Tree creates a shelter with arms and legs on floor,*) and the tree/shelter closed its doors and closed its windows. (*'Tree' body closes in to protect child*)

During the night there were lots of noises in the forest (*noises made by trees*), but the creatures were quite safe. The next morning, when the sun was up, the trees opened their doors and the small creatures stretched themselves and opened their eyes. They peered out of the windows and decided to explore the forest. They came out of the shelter and decided to climb the tree (*'tree' acts as climbing frame for child to climb to hip or shoulders*) and looked out into the forest.

In the distance, the creatures could see some water and decided to go looking for food and drink. They climbed down from the tree and left their shelter and went off together.

The above story is much more advanced than the previous ones: everyone is in role as tree/shelter or animal, although the emphasis is on movement. Movement is more detailed as opposed to the gross movement of the earlier stories; there is also more interaction. There is a range of responses required – tiredness, choices (which house?), trust (being looked after), support (solid climbing tree) and separation (leaving home again). The story also places more imaginative demands on the children. They are working first as two differentiated groups (although they remain individual within the group) – trees/shelters and small animals – and then in pairs, contrasting in each group – one carer and one cared for – and then differentiated into groups of individuals.

ELABORATIONS

There are creatures in the forest and the small animals take one or all of the following courses of action:

- Go out to explore and then return to the safety of the tree/shelter
- Decide to live in the forest
- Find one magic creature in the forest who gives them a secret.

I was asked to work with a mixed group of children with learning disabilities. Originally I was expecting to work with six to nine year olds, but when I arrived I was asked to take an integrated class which included ten to thirteen-year-olds. (The older children were so large!) I decided to use the magic forest story and ask the older children to be the trees/shelters. I told the story as it is given above. The older children made very realistic forest sounds, yet were very protective of the small animals. I decided that there should be the sounds of a creature in the forest that might be good or might be bad and that the small animals were going to discover what it was.

The children set off the 'next morning' and found a magic cat which had been trapped by a witch, and they knew the magic word ('doughnuts') to set it free. The cat then joined their group and went off on the journey.

After we had finished, I was going to build another episode on to the story, but the older children said, 'It's our turn now. We want to be the little animals'. The younger children then became the trees and were literally 'stretched' as these lumbering lads and tall girls (all of them big for their age) curled up in their shelters.

The teacher later told me that this was the first time the older children had ever done anything where they might feel silly and that they had never done any dramatic play before.

The Under-, Over- and Distortedly-Held Child

When children are what I refer to as *under-held, over-held* or *distortedly-held*, they will not flourish and may develop severe impairment.

The Under-Held Child

The under-held child is:

- neglected
- left alone for long periods
- not stimulated

- not affirmed
- often fails to thrive
- may become non-responsive and lethargic.

The child who is not held enough develops neither a sense of security and support nor a sense of *body-self.* A child needs to experience its body-self before it can develop a body-image.

The following extended case history serves as an example of a situation where the child's early experience was severely impoverished.

Bobby, aged two, had been referred by his health visitor who was worried about his development; it turned out that there had also been an enquiry from the parents concerning finding foster parents for him as they considered him handicapped. While the situation was being considered, it was thought that the special nursery could provide some relief for the parents, as well as some stimulus for the child.

When I arrived to visit the family, his mother was very anxious and wanted to tell me everything that they had done in order to be good parents. The house was spotless and I was offered a cup of coffee. Afterwards the cup was immediately seized and washed up. It was difficult to get the mother to sit and relax while she talked with me. Her story seemed very sad. She and her husband had met through their work in computing and had started playing squash together regularly. They had similar interests in work and sport and so had married, thinking that one day a baby might be a nice idea.

The baby arrived after two years, and, the mother went on to say: 'That's when all the problems started. We never thought having a baby would create such a terrible problem. It has really ruined our lives – and we had a good life. It doesn't seem fair. I think the whole idea of having babies is pretty disgusting anyway. I asked the doctor if I could have a full anaesthetic so I didn't know what was happening. He said they would only do that if it was a Caesarean and that might be the case since I have small hips – so I was banking on that. And David and I agreed that he should wait at home till it was all over. I didn't want him to see me in any sort of mess. Anyway, I had the operation, so didn't come round until I had the stitches and everything done, and one underweight bundle was put into my lap. Of course I didn't want to feed, so there was all the routine of the bottles and mixing and everything. The nurses did it in the hospital and then I had to do it when they sent me home a week later. They kept saying he had to put on weight, so I had to keep feeding him all times of the night and day. I tried to get him on a routine, but I couldn't stand the crying. Whenever he cries, I just stick something in his mouth. I've been at home with him all this time, just clearing up and washing and bathing. It's a full-time job, and I don't like it. I want to go back to work: I want to play squash again with my husband. I'm worried that my figure has gone to seed now that I'm not exercising. He still goes, and there are plenty of young trim women at the club. And I'm terrified of having another baby – so every month I get anxious.'

As she told me this in an almost non-stop monologue, she sat there screwing a handkerchief around her fingers and fighting hard to keep her tears back. She did not appear to have 'gone to seed' and indeed looked immaculate. I felt that it was not the place to explore the various levels of what she was saying (gone to seed?) but I also felt that she and her husband needed some help. I said that I should see Bobby and then we could have a chat about possible options she and her husband might like to consider.

She led me to a space at the foot of the stairs – a space about four feet square that had been fenced off, with guard-rails in the doorway to any rooms and to the stairs. There was polythene lining the floor and a blue blanket placed over it. Bobby was sitting in a corner, totally placid, sucking his thumb. His mother immediately removed his thumb from his mouth, saying, 'I've told you before – stop that!' Inside the 'cage' were three balloons, a small teddy-bear, and a cushion. Bobby was overweight and continued to sit throughout.

When I asked if Bobby could walk yet, she replied that that was why they had realised he was handicapped, because he could not walk, feed himself, or do anything for himself, and he was not clean or dry. I asked if we could take him out of the play-pen and she fetched me a 'pinny' to keep my clothes clean; she then lifted him up, holding him at a distance, and passed him to me. We returned to the kitchen and sat down. Bobby sat still on my lap, looked at his mother and put a hand out, saying 'urhh, urhh'. She brought a high chair with a harness out of the cupboard, put Bobby into it, tied a full-length bib onto him, and proceeded to give him a drink from a beaker with a spout while she held his arms away. The telephone rang and she went to answer it whereupon the child promptly grasped the beaker for himself and started to drink: there was no problem of his not knowing what to do.

When she returned, I suggested that Bobby started at the nursery three mornings a week; that he would be fetched and brought back; and asked if she would send some play-clothes in case the children got messy.

She winced at this, but said she would like him to attend while they were exploring the possibility of fostering.

Bobby started at the nursery the following week, and arrived with a brand new set of overalls for messy play. He was quite overwhelmed by the level of noise and people, and we allotted one of the workers to be with him all the time and to introduce him gradually to the various activities. After a couple of weeks, he was assessed and found to have normal intelligence, but to be functioning at roughly the level of an eighteen-month-old due to under-stimulation and *lack of physical bonding.*

His parents did manage to have him fostered, and eventually he was adopted into a family with two children who were very boisterous and physical. He continued at the nursery where he progressed through a developmental programme of movement and play where the early stages of embodiment were re-experienced. The foster parents were involved in the whole programme, reinforcing the work at the nursery. Bobby was allowed to regress in his movement with constant rocking and cradling; games with rolling, pulling and pushing across the floor; building shelters with people; and being able to climb and explore. He soon pulled himself up to a walking position and walked independently within three months.

Bobby's speech was very slow to develop and he tried to get everything he wanted by making noises and pointing. The staff quickly realised that this behaviour was inhibiting further speech. They designed a play programme for all the children which involved a range of sounds and use of the breath. The important thing to note here is that, with Bobby, it was important to start from the *early* bodily stages, those that Bobby had not experienced in his family.

(Although Bobby's parents were offered the support of marital therapy, they declined, saying that everything was fine now that Bobby was in a foster home. They readily agreed to his adoption, and did not have any more children; in fact his mother told the health visitor that she was waiting for sterilisation.)

As can be seen from the above example, this child's development was seriously affected by the lack of physical contact with adults, and, additionally, by the lack of stimulation both from parents and from the environment – in his case what I call a 'soft' environment.

I give this as an example of the child who is *under-held.* Deprived of physical contact, the child does not develop a sense of body-self or the ability to achieve normal landmarks in physical mastery. In fact, infants who are not held usually become lethargic and depressed, a state that is mistaken by many parents as 'being good'.

The Over-Held Child

The child who is over-held:

- is over-protected
- is not stimulated
- is not encouraged to risk-take
- has difficulty becoming independent
- is often frightened of exploring.

This state may occur when there has been difficulty at birth, or difficulty in conceiving in the first place, or if a child is premature, ill or disabled. Sometimes the child still represents the 'dream baby' – becoming what the parents have longed for – and is smothered with care and attention like a love object rather than being encouraged as an individual in its own right. The smothering love is different from the holding, nurturing and exploration of touch that *all children need*. All children need additional *holding*, where the child is just held, stroked and massaged, quite apart from the holding involved in attending to the bodily needs of feeding and cleaning.

If parents have difficulties during the conception stage (Jennings 1992a) and the resultant child has arrived after lengthy treatments and periods of waiting, it can be difficult for them to allow the child to develop autonomy. An example which illustrates this is that of the parent who wakes up every two hours in order to check that their child is still breathing.

It is not easy for any parent to gauge the appropriate balance between nurture and independence. Nurture consists not only of responses to bodily functions, as in feeding and cleaning, but also of the *emotional* need to be held, massaged and stroked. It is this very way of holding that becomes smothering when the parent is doing it for their own needs rather than the needs of the child. Once again there needs to be a balance because, obviously, parents have needs too, and one way they are satisfied is in engagement with the child.

An extreme example of over-holding can be illustrated by the practice of wrapping small babies in tight swaddling clothes; although these provide close containment on the one hand, they allow absolutely no bodily movement on the other.

'Screaming Charlie' is a good example of the over-held child – the child's nickname was given to him by neighbours and relatives when Charlie, aged two, was allowed to scream for whatever he wanted until it was given to him.

> Charlie was conceived after a series of miscarriages over a five-year period. His mother was ordered bed-rest – yet again – when she conceived for the sixth time. Although there were some signs of bleeding, this time the pregnancy continued and Charlie was born, six weeks premature, and spent his first two weeks in an incubator. His mother stayed at the hospital day and night and when she took Charlie home, he became the entire focus of her life. Not only did he have very frequent medical check-ups and second opinions but he was never allowed out of his mother's sight.
>
> Her husband coped for a few months but soon drifted away into a more immediate relationship when he was no longer able to engage with his wife or, indeed, have relaxed access with his son. Without her husband as a mediating factor, Charlie's mother was able to devote even more time to the beloved child and he grew up in an atmosphere of total attention, sterilised food and toys, and a hovering anxiety that something might be wrong.
>
> The family's GP suggested that Charlie might benefit from nursery school and, after much reluctance, his mother allowed him to try; however, the staff eventually had to ask her to leave with her son because she would not stay away herself and cross-examined the staff on their hygiene, food, and so on. Charlie had not yet developed socially at all and was unable to engage in playing. He was eventually referred by the GP for psychological assessment after the teacher at his primary school said he was still functioning at the level of a two-year-old. Charlie was referred for playtherapy but it was quickly realised that the most important thing was to get appropriate referral for his mother. She did enter psychotherapy and went through a period of playtherapy herself in order to help him make the bridges into more mature ways of behaving.

Without wishing to enter the one-parent/two-parent debate, in this situation it seems clear that Charlie's father may well have been a mediating factor and even have helped to bring about change if early enough support could have been obtained for the family as a whole.

In such a situation one can only welcome the enlightened insistence of the GP – otherwise Charlie could well have ended up in long-term therapy for a situation that needed his mother to change. Charlie was later helped to handle his need for independence in a realistic way. The screaming bouts ceased to occur after the first therapy session.

Distorted Holding

Let us now consider the child who has been inappropriately or violently held – the more extreme versions of the under or over-held child. Here, I wish to set out some guidelines for body-play when physical abuse is suspected or proven.

Some workers feel uncomfortable with the idea of body-play with children who have suffered body trauma. They often in fact focus on the telling of what happened rather than on the repair and re-parenting that is necessary.

Although the results of over or under-holding may be compensated for and redressed later in life, distorted embodiment experiences often take much longer to treat and may cause permanent damage if the problem is not diagnosed in childhood. The following are examples of distorted holding:

- physical abuse, that is, blows
- sexual abuse – exploration and/or penetration
- physical neglect
- lack of safety, for example, dropping the child
- distorted feeding.

In small infants, such holding often does not come to light unless there is non-accidental injury or it has been noticed that the child does not thrive. The worst types of cases often end with the death of a child and/or a court case. However, it may be that a child does survive and is treated, when he or she is older, in therapy. Although such distortions may permanently damage a child, recall before the age of two years is rare in most children.

Often the emphasis in treatment is too much on attempted disclosure rather than the repair and re-parenting that is needed to provide a nurturing embodiment experience. Work with the body is important to re-establish touch, trust, and later creativity. This process may take a long time and, for the child who has suffered undue violence, requires working and waiting with patience.

Frequently such a child needs more personal space – that is the space that surrounds him or her – and as workers we need to be sensitive to this and gauge the proximity to another human being that the child can tolerate. The space between child and adult can be bridged through the use of woven materials – long strips of chiffon, for example, that can help establish contact without being invasive. Safety can also be established by allowing the child to create a 'home base' with a large hoop, play-mat or large cushion. This creation of the 'larger space' to institute a layer of protection can be compared to the obese person who creates a similar safety layer, using their own body.

Ultimately the aim of all interventions is to assist the child to re-experience nurturing and boisterous play as safe occupations that can be enjoyed without fear of violence. The child may also need to play through the violence he or she has actually experienced and there are many different ways of doing this.

Repair and Re-Parenting

In the case of the over-held child, he or she is likely to be very dependent as well as to have problems separating from the mother. Such a child will also be under-stimulated in terms of the expanding world and have a fear of exploration and risk.

The under-held child will not have experienced primary nurturing and is likely to be depressed, lethargic and without a developed body-self. If the child is stimulated out of its lethargy, it may well be anxious, nervous, hyperactive, clumsy and have lack of attention span.

The child who has experienced distorted holding will have a chaotic experience of his or her own body and no sense of body-self.

This chapter has focused on the first stage, Embodiment, of the EPR developmental paradigm. It includes sensory play, movement play and movement stories, and illustrations of application with children.

Whereas I emphasise the importance of establishing trust between child and therapist, this may not necessarily mean physical touch. For many children touch may have been a traumatic experience, especially where physical violence and sexual abuse is concerned.

Finally, may I make a plea for more understanding of cross-cultural values? The human body carries cultural metaphors through which deeply embedded beliefs are expressed (see Jennings 1995c). The body is a primary means of expression.

'Ladies have big boobies because the babies press inside them and stretch it.'
(Harry, aged four)

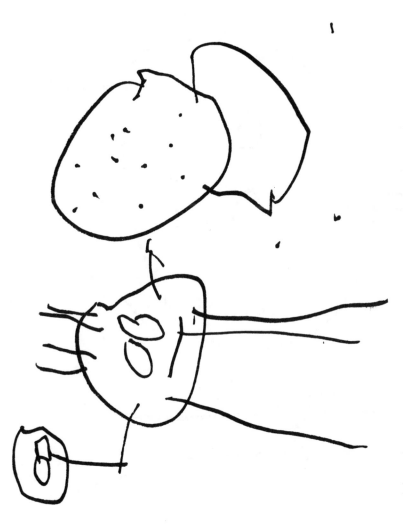

'The monster and the castle with a garden. There are apples on the tree and blood coming out if his mouth' by George, aged 3½

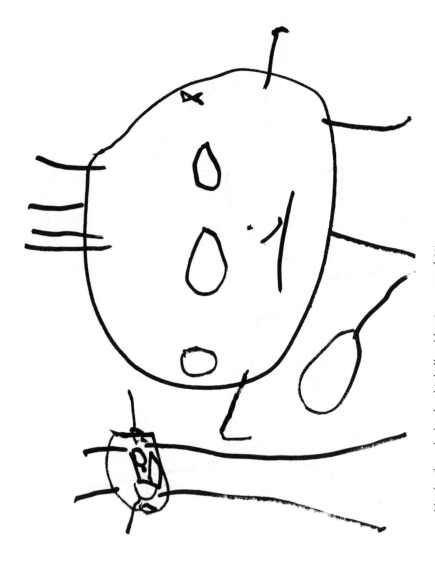

'The sad monster and his brother who has lost his balloon' by George, aged 3½

CHAPTER 6

Practical Playtherapy: Projection

Bassanio: Here in her hairs
The painter plays the spider.

(The Merchant of Venice, III, ii, 120–121*)*

As the young child increasingly develops the capacity to pretend we can observe an increase in projective and symbolic play. Objects can become toys; for example, a brick can become a house or a lorry, an animal can take on human characteristics. The child is projecting ideas and feelings into the toys and objects around. As we have already seen the stage of Projection is part of normal human development. Projective play can be exploratory, sensory and manipulative. In therapy a child may need to learn or re-learn the capacity to play with and through various media. The child may need to spend a lot of exploratory time before symbolising his or her experiences through projective play.

Just as the child who has been deprived of bodily experience during the Embodiment stage may need to re-experience and re-learn the 'body world', a child may also need to re-experience sensory and exploratory play in order to play projectively.

It is important in the range of toys that are available for projective play that they cover a wide range of scale. Toys need to be smaller and much smaller than a child as well as larger than the child. It is essential to remember that what seems miniature to an adult may seem only a little bit smaller to the child. Generally children are intrigued by very small toys and they give them an opportunity to exercise control over their world rather than being overwhelmed with epic size experiences. Children also become absorbed in toys that fit inside themselves which takes us into the whole question of containment. The sensory and texture boxes, described in Chapter 5, set limits for the child's borders. Similarly, different toy boxes, the sand tray and 'container' toys provide security and borders to the child's experience. Part of the closure of a session can be the dismantling of the toys and objects and returning them to their boxes.

I have used the following miniature toys extensively with children and grown-ups alike:

- Punch and Judy with dog and baby
- Noah's ark with several pairs of animals
- Baby dragon emerging from an egg
- Guatemalan worry dolls
- Various finger puppets.

Many of these toys already come in small boxes or we can find trinket tins and boxes that can contain individual toys. They are all small enough to explore with safety an experience that feels too large to deal with. A variation of projective techniques using small toys includes, of course, the Lowenfeld World technique mentioned in Chapter 1.

A playtherapist can make use of as much choice of toys as possible, but can I emphasise the importance of not always getting 'designer' equipment. Many children gain more from a blanket draped over a table than they do from an expensive Wendy house. Large cardboard boxes such as those which contain freezers or televisions, large paper sacks, blankets and large nesting boxes are all necessary for what I term 'Container Play'. Children in therapy often need more than just the safety of the playtherapy room and the playtherapist. They want to create a space within a space where they can hide or talk or create stories or dramas. Some children may spend a long time under the blankets, recreating a safe bed, especially if their own bed is a dangerous one.

Toys of all shapes and sizes and from many different cultures can be used to create scenes, tell stories and portray events. The advantage of toys is that they are mobile and can be re-arranged, unlike painting, which becomes a fixed picture.

There are also other toys which are made up as something inside something, inside something else, which have particular playtherapy methods associated with them. The best known is the Russian Babushka doll where several peasant women, carved in wood (there are also other ethnic variations and viking dolls) are contained one within the other down to a very small size. The dolls are usually at least five in number and may be many more. Children and adults are captivated by these dolls and may spend much time examining and arranging them in different ways. There are several ways of using Babushka:

- to explore the dynamics of the members of the family
- to externalise the different people the child feels are inside the self
- to create the ideal family: 'how I would like it to be'
- to explore issues around new babies and siblings
- to tell stories with the dolls providing the starting point.

Playtherapists will find that children spontaneously make use of Babushka in many different ways, often guiding a therapist through a scene.

Mary had taken all the dolls out from the Babushka and stood them in a group. She examined each, talking to herself as she did so: 'Hmmm, this is a fat one, it must be the mother; this is auntie and she and mummy have a row... the little girl starts to cry so her big sister takes her to play outside ...the auntie goes home because she is crying ... And mummy cooks the tea ...'

During this time, Mary moved the dolls around as if they were puppets and the grouping of four dolls went from being altogether to the two smaller ones being placed at one end of the table, the 'aunt' under the table, and the 'mother' at the other end. It was only then that I realised that Mary was playing with four Babushkas and that the smallest was nowhere to be seen. I gave a gentle prompt and said, 'What happens then?'

As if I hadn't spoken, Mary continued her story.

The fat mummy has got to go into hospital so she has to call the auntie back again ... Come here stupid woman ... You must look after these children ... the ambulance is coming ...'[1]

She brought the 'aunt' back again who called the children in from the garden and gave them tea, and they waved to mummy who was going to hospital.

'The mummy went to the hospital to have a baby... The baby was dead ... So mummy came home without it ... And she and the auntie both cried.'

She took the smallest Babushka from inside the large one:

'The baby's got to be buried.'

She fetched some sand in a small plastic bowl.

'You must be buried because you're dead.'

She picked up two small dolls and said:

'... And the girls cry because the baby is dead and they haven't got a new sister.'

She looked up and said:

'That's the end.'

This was a multi-layered statement for a small child dealing with a bereavement that had not been explained to her.

The baby had died within minutes of birth and the mother had 'dealt' with everything at the hospital before she had returned home. She did not think it important for the two daughters to be involved in the brief funeral service and had not shared anything with her children.

For many children the making of marks on paper can be very scary because it involves a commitment. There may be children who would initially prefer to play around with toys than actually to draw or paint something. However there are children who would not dream of playing with toys and who see drawing and painting as more adult activities. It is all to do with the fine tuning of the therapist's intuition, if indeed intuition is something you can tune! Perhaps what I mean is that the therapist needs a wide-angle lens and to be in a state of readiness in order to pick up the child's cues.

A child will often say, 'What shall I draw?' and expect a direction from the therapist. Unless the playtherapist is using a specific technique, such as the rosebush exercise, or the monster technique, the child feels there is a lot of unspoken expectation of what they will produce. One child said to me, 'I can't draw anything' so I said, 'Well, just draw nothing', and she promptly created a 'nothing' picture. The child also needs to know what will happen to the picture and indeed will often ask the therapist to look after it, because it might be destroyed at home. Often I find that humming or singing during drawing and painting, and also with the use of play dough and plasticine, helps people to be less self-conscious.

> Liz has no memory of any abuse. Her mother told her that when she went to the shops she'd heard her daughter scream 'No, No, No'. Her mother looked over the balcony and saw a man disappearing. Her daughter was crying and when her mother came she told her she had been asked to do something naughty. Her mother rang the police. Liz was referred for playtherapy at the age of twelve after increasingly disruptive outbursts at school, together with truanting and stealing. She came to the first session and presented as tough and self-sufficient and told me not to 'make' her do anything, and then she said she would just like to have a chat. She said how important it was for her not to be weak and that she must never be caught out and no one must get the better of her. I showed her the technique of 'life maps' and 'life lines' which have signposts, roads, paths, stop/go, buildings and landscapes. She got into the habit of drawing maps while she was 'chatting' and her maps had their own logic as well as being symbolic. She drew a tower block of flats and said 'I was six when all that happened, and this road leads to the police station'. Her description of her examination by the police doctor was dramatic. 'My mum screamed and carried me into the flats and rang the police and said I had been attacked. A car arrived, sirens blazing and mum said a man on the playground had attacked me. They sent a policeman to look for him and took us to the station – everything was in such a hurry and people were panicking – they made me lie on the bed – there were lots of bright lights and the doctor examined me – and these other people held me down because I was screaming.'

We can see that she is describing a secondary abuse in very clear detail. In a later session she said how much she regretted moving from the house where they used to live which they did because her mother was sure that her attacker was a man who lived nearby. Suddenly Liz said that she did remember and said that a boy had come up to her and asked her to take down her knickers so he could have a look. She had shouted 'no' and he had run away. Liz was certain it was a teenage boy from the next street, while her mother was sure it was a man. The mother insisted that they move to where nobody knew them in order 'to make a fresh start'. She was fetched from school one day to go to the new house and hadn't even been told they were moving.

These sessions with Liz shortly after she started her new secondary school demonstrate how a somewhat unconventional, though structured, approach allowed her to retrieve significant memories. She was able to express real sadness at leaving the tower block of flats and the people that she knew in her environment. The dramatic and panicked reactions of the adults in Liz's world had blocked what had actually happened to her and her anger was far greater at being moved without warning to a new place than at the events preceding it.

Disruption or Absence of Projective Play

Disruption of Normal Development

Children who have been hospitalised for severe illness or disability may well miss out on these important stages of play development, although it is encouraging to see that many more hospitals set great store by the work of play teachers and nursery nurses. It may also be in some situations that families, or rather parents, do not see the value of the play experiences, and will discourage play. They may see this as a short-cut to encourage a child to become an adult as quickly as possible; they may also place themselves in the role of teacher and direct their children's play. Others believe in encouraging the total freedom of the child and expect them 'to go and play', the sub-text of this being 'don't get in the way'.

There is still some ambivalence in western culture about play and the word can be used in a pejorative sense. Teachers and educationalists are therefore often hard-pressed to explain to parents the importance of play, both for its own sake, and as a precursor to other forms of learning.

Absence of Projective Play

Where there is a great emphasis on academic or professional achievement in a family, there can be a denial of the importance of play. This phenomenon is not confined to the professional classes: I have seen it as much with working-class families who wish for something better for their children, as with professional and academic families. Often children of four and five years of age have enormous pressure put on them for academic achievement, with private tuition, educational videos and home-time programmed for formal learning. It is difficult for some parents to understand that the seeming time-wasting of 'play' will in itself develop a child's skills and intelligence.

> Lena came to see me about her thirteen-year-old son whom she described as a delinquent. Lena came from Cyprus, had married a British soldier, and had two sons – Nikos, sixteen, and Johnnie, thirteen. She described her older son as successful and intelligent; her younger son on the other hand was a worry, kept her awake at nights, and would, she thought, come to a bad end. When I asked her to describe what Johnnie did, she burst into tears and said that she didn't know what to do. The main problem as she saw it was that he would not do his homework and always wanted to play football. 'I've gone out working to pay for extra classes,' she said, 'I've tried so hard to be a good mother and provide him with things'.
>
> Lena wanted both her sons to go to university and to have professions, perhaps as doctors or lawyers. She felt that she herself had been deprived of a good education and that her husband, 'a good man', was only a soldier. This wasn't good enough for her boys and she was determined to provide them with better chances. Her husband did not figure much in these decisions, but supported her. He was away a lot but was always a dutiful husband and father.
>
> Johnnie wasted his chances, she said, by wanting to play outside all the time, even pretending to have done his homework when he hadn't: 'He's lying to me – lying; so now I test him on everything when he says he's done it. Why should he lie to me? He will be a delinquent.'
>
> It turned out that Johnnie had had private tuition from the age of six in reading and mathematics. Her struggle with him had been going on for several years to make him work. At school he was often referred to as 'a dreamer', and although he had not made brilliant academic progress, nevertheless he was not causing any concern; however, they had been disappointed that he had not been allowed to take a place in the sports team.
>
> At this initial interview I suggested to Lena that she tried a compromise with her son in order to try and take the heat out of the

situation. In the end we agreed that he could play football immediately after school, either at school or at home, and then would do his homework after he had had his supper. We also agreed that he would do only the homework set by the school and not any extra for two weeks.

The school indicated that they could contain the situation without singling Johnnie out for individual therapy. They encouraged him in his sports and gave him feedback about the satisfactory standard of his academic work.

Lena came to see me again three weeks later, still a worried mother, but less 'on the boil'. I did not consider therapy to be necessary for her but she did need some help to understand ordinary adolescence and also to enable her to build a world for herself. She was able to tell me that she was very lonely in England and that her sole focus was her children. We had three sessions of talking together, looking at her own needs and at the importance of expanding her world. Johnnie continued to develop as a healthy teenager, infinitely more confident once he was both allowed and encouraged to play football.

In this example we may note how important it is to have an understanding of cultural norms and values. Contemporary Greek society places tremendous importance on early academic learning and achievement. This in Lena's case was exacerbated by her loneliness and isolation and at times by 'culture clash'.

Directed Play

With some children, parents (and teachers too) feel that their play activity should be directed by the adult. The child is praised for reproducing what the adult wants from him or her. A child's endeavours will be paraded in front of other relatives, and experimentation is dismissed as 'silly' or 'nonsense'. The fundamental point that a child makes sense through nonsense is not understood. Such children are allowed to play with construction sets and other toys which are seen as highly educational with a purpose; painting is by numbers and not allowed to be free; accuracy and reproduction through copying and tracing is praised and anything that might be a muddle, messy or dirty is discouraged. Toys are often miniature reproductions of adult objects: these include specific dressing-up clothes, toy dustpans and brushes, a designer Wendy house and so on. Such parents become very daunted and even hurt when a child takes more pleasure in the box and wrapping in which the present arrived or when the child spends pocket-money on a box of old buttons at a jumble sale.

While it is true that one of the functions of play is to play out adult situations and roles and pastimes that children will encounter later in life, what is being missed is that the child's own imaginative and problem-solving resources are not being developed. Rigid play is likely to develop rigid people, and those children who have not developed their own resources are likely to have difficulties in dealing with new and unexpected situations. It is through our capacity to be creative that we learn to deal with life itself. The child who is unable to play projectively in symbolic form is deprived of the capacity to struggle with the world and to make sense of it. All it receives is the adult's view of the world through a very restricted telescope.

Projective Play with No Limits

In some child development and family beliefs, there is a school of thought that suggests the child should be allowed to develop with no intervention from adults: playing should be a completely free activity, and in this way the child will learn all that is ever needed. This approach is the antithesis of the previous description of rigid play and can be equally stultifying to the child's growth. A child needs adults to be involved in play from time to time. From ten months old, the child will make the adult into an audience to watch performances. Children need adults to join in the struggle sometimes: to play *with* them, rather than to do it *for* them. Children also need adults to be able to set limits and boundaries to contain the play – the well-known 'tears before bedtime' situation.

A child who does not have an adult to play with for some of the time, will only play within its own experience or will create an experience with no boundaries, something that can be very frightening. Play needs to be both solitary, adult-shared, and social – where others are true participants within the play, and not silent on-lookers or absent figures.

Projective Methods

Projective Play in Therapy

I now want to concentrate on the use of projective play in symbolic play when it is being used for diagnostic, exploratory and reparative intervention. We shall see how this can be achieved through recreation and new formulation of old structures where children are empowered to intervene in

their life patterns. The methods described below form the basis of much dramatherapy work, particularly of what is known as 'sculpting', where clients of all ages make use of their capacity to project as a way of looking at their lives and life decisions and at the possibility of new outcomes.

The well-equipped playtherapy room includes a varied range of projective materials which may be used in directive and non-directive ways. These include animals of all sorts (domestic and wild), trees, gates, cars, aeroplanes, shells, stones, twigs, nesting dolls. The play must have some physical boundaries quite apart from the boundaries set by time and room-space and by the basic rules. Projective play may thus be carried out on a tray, a sand box, a small table, a piece of sugar paper or a rug, for example. Not to provide these boundaries can create an experience that is very overwhelming for the child. Physical boundaries, as we have said, act as a container for the experience. The child is invited to create a picture or to tell a story using the materials to hand. The child may do this spontaneously or may respond to an invitation. The child who is ready to tell his or her story will not need any coaxing or commanding – provided the atmosphere is safe and the materials are appropriate.

The following is a description of a sculpt created by Trevor, a child who had been sexually abused.

> He placed a heap of twigs and leaves in one corner of the tray; a rhinoceros, an elephant and a small dog in a row in descending order of size; lots of other toy animals in heaps and groups mixed together and not standing up; then some stones and trees at intervals.
>
> Trevor said: 'It's the dog's story and the dog is unhappy because of the big animals'. I asked if this was the rhinoceros and the elephant. Trevor replied 'Mmm, the 'oceros is big and scary and the elephant can't see but the dog can, and all the other animals can't see so the dog wants to hide and hides by the tree and the 'oceros says 'I'm coming to get you' and the dog hates it and cries'.
>
> At this point he started to cry and changed to the first person and continued: 'I hate him, hate him'.
>
> He grabbed the rhinoceros and flung it away. He had a heightened colour and looked momentarily relieved.
>
> The temptation at a moment like this is to lead the child into disclosure work about details of the actual abuse. However, this is not a

disclosure interview, and it is crucial to follow the child, if necessary with a prompt such as 'and what happens next in the story?' or 'what did the dog do then'. On this occasion the child continued without a prompt and said: 'The dog had to keep finding new places to hide and not play the monster game, and the trees weren't big enough, so in the end (and he looked up with triumph and glee) the dog found the rubbish tip and the monster couldn't find him'.

He placed the dog underneath the pile of leaves and twigs.

I asked him if the dog felt quite safe in the rubbish tip. He replied 'Nobody knows the tip because it's just a lot of rubbish, so nobody goes there, except the dog'. He looked at the picture for a few moments and then said 'That's the end of the story; goodbye'.

I said 'So that's the end of the story and the dog feels quite safe in the rubbish tip'. 'Yes' said Trevor, 'let's do something else now'. 'OK' I replied, 'but let's put this story away first, and then you choose what you want to do next'.

Just as pictures and stories can be created, they must also be dismantled, and it is important that the children, where possible, do this for themselves. It is a means of transforming the play materials into their general state again and diffusing the intensity with which they have been invested during the playtherapy.

Here, the materials are being 'de-roled', as in a piece of drama work, and the process should not be hurried. It is not a question of tidying them away, but of allowing them to become neutral again, ready for any future work.

After this story and the de-roling, Trevor wanted to play very boisterously in the soft corner with cushions and soft toys. 'I'm going to bury you', he said.

He proceeded to pile the cushions and toys on top of me. 'You can breathe, can't you?' he asked.

The answer he seemed to anticipate was 'yes', and in any case I could breathe perfectly well. 'Yes, I can breathe' I replied.

He piled more cushions. 'Can you now?' he asked again.

I was beginning to get very uncomfortable and was pretty sure that he was using me to test something for himself. I pushed my head out and said: 'It's getting difficult to breathe'. So he said, 'You do that to me now'.

I piled a few things, and asked 'Can you breathe now?' 'Course I can, put lots more on!' he said.

I added a few cushions and asked 'Can you breathe now?' 'Yes, put lots more! ...'

I added some more cushions and toys and said, 'That's it; I'm not putting any more there. No, that's enough; we'll stop while you can still breathe.'

There was a pause, and then Trevor said, 'All right then. You be the monster and make no noise'.

I thought he had said 'and make a noise', so I replied: 'What sort of noise?' 'No noise' he said, 'you are a silent monster'.

I crouched outside the cushions and said very quietly: 'I am a silent monster and I don't make any noise. The creature in the cushions can't hear me because I don't make any noise!'

Gradually there was movement in the pile of cushions and Trevor slowly emerged, obviously not wanting to be seen by the monster, so I did not look at him. He held up a cushion and brought it down on my back and said: 'The monster is dead. Go on, make a dying noise'.

I provided some suitable moans and groans and then 'expired'. He went a few paces away and took a flying leap, landing on the cushions.

He said, 'You see; the monster is dead, he can't even make dead noises now, or quiet ones'. I told him 'It's time to stop now, so I am going to be me again and not the monster'.

As I sat up, he looked very satisfied and said: 'Good story, isn't it? I want to do it again next time'.

The above stories could be interpreted in many different ways, depending on the reader's particular orientation. Perhaps a useful exercise would be to try analysing the stories from Freudian, Jungian, Kleinian and Piagetian viewpoints. However, try to consider also what it meant for the child in the here and now.

Let us look at the two stories, both – as it turned out – using different projective techniques, in terms of what the child wanted to do.

In the sculpt, Trevor created a representation of how the abusive situation felt, the rhinoceros father, elephant mother and dog-child being the main protagonists. The heaps of other animals were other adults who 'never see'; trees and stones were not big enough to hide in, and the rubbish tip was the safe place.

It is crucial at this point that the therapist not only *sees* what the child needs to be seen but also hears what the child wants to be heard. The picture enabled me to see his own view of his situation. There are many themes, the dominant themes being:

- people not seeing (others in the child's environment)
- 'monster games' from which he could not escape
- a place of safety, in this case the rubbish tip.

In fact, the child had spelled out his needs more clearly than could be done in any case conference, through his projective play.

Within the play he is already attempting to change the outcome of the monster game that he cannot escape. He is able to fling the rhinoceros away and thereby take control. It is important to pace oneself with the child. For example, a therapist might have been tempted to pursue the above picture and look at the people who had not seen and the people who (presumably) now did see. What was the role of the mother in all this? How might the elephant be developed in the picture? This might be appropriate for future work, but at this time the child was self-directing and made it clear when he wanted to end the story. My own intervention was purely to allow the ending, that is, the de-roling of the toys, so that they could become neutral again.

The same child himself directed the next story, and this time wanted me to be a part of it. I was to be the 'no-noise monster' that he was able to destroy. Again, it was important for him to feel in control and change the outcome himself. In the first part of the story, when he asked me to be buried in the cushions, again it would have been easy to interpret rather than to deal with his actual needs. The cushions, for example, could represent the womb and the emergence – the birth experience – but this does not seem to be an explanation that furthered whatever the child needed to address. He continued piling cushions onto me until I imposed a limit and he was then able to demonstrate that he could tolerate even more cushions than I could. In fact, he wanted me to pile on yet more, but again I set a limit. It was not clear at this time how much the cushions represented the actual abuse with an adult's weight crushed on top of him and him not being able to breathe. It could also portray his fear of dying. What was obvious was that the cushions could become the safe place, like the rubbish tip, from which he could emerge to kill the silent monster.

In reflection afterwards I thought that perhaps silent monsters are more scary than noisy ones. The ordinary 'I'm coming to get you' games can turn out to be far more sinister and even sadistic.

As the child's world expands, so do the means whereby, and through which, the child can play. Already in the above case history example we can see how the second story began to involve the therapist 'in role'.

Projective Media

Earlier in this chapter I listed a range of projective materials for use in playtherapy. However modest the budget, the important thing is to have some contrast and choices between, for example, messy and non-messy play (finger paints and felt pens), between concrete and symbolic toys (family dolls and animal families).

Sensory Projective Play

Play with sand and water and finger paint acts as one of the bridges between the Embodiment and Projection stages, and children who are deprived of sensory experiences need plenty of time to experiment and explore. This can be a time of sheer wonder and magic.

WATER PLAY

Use washing-up bowls with contrasting temperatures of water to develop sensory awareness through the child splashing, feeling, trickling and all the other experiences associated with 'water words'; elaborate the play with bubbles as well as containers, funnels and so on.

This is a clear example of where the 'educational' and the 'therapeutic' overlap and in my view it is entirely relevant to enable the playtherapist to encourage sensory 'repair' play. It is also worth noting that children with 'bed-wetting' problems have, through this play, been able to control their physical body through being able to control water *outside of themselves.*

SAND AND WATER PLAY

Ideally, have a tray of wet and a tray of dry sand – larger washing-up bowls can be used but are rather deep; alternatively, cat litter trays can be used since they are about the right size if rather shallow. The wet and dry sand can be experienced for its own sake – some sand can be controlled and some not. Sand can also be used to build landscapes, buildings and other structures.

It is very important for the child to play with 'natural substances' such as sand and water to which may be added stones, shells, twigs, leaves, grasses and so on. Such play allows primary sensation.

CREATING OR SCULPTING THE STORY OR SCENE

The most detailed method here is the Lowenfeld World Technique (1935) where the child chooses from a vast array of toys and objects. However, the child may also be enabled to tell the projective story with modest numbers of small toys, objects (including natural ones) and a wet sand tray.

As has been emphasised throughout this book, playtherapists must be careful not to impose their own view of the child's story. The sculpted picture in the sand tray may be the first time that the child has been able to articulate his or her own life crisis and what is needed is the therapist's attention. A child will so easily share his or her story in this way that we must beware of being 'predators', especially as we find some images 'interesting'.

FINGER PAINT PLAY

An A4 piece of paper is usually large enough for finger painting. There should be a choice of paint colours. Children who have been kept obsessively clean will often avoid something so messy. However there is usually a progression from using one finger to using both hands. The child will create shapes and patterns and sometimes incorporate toys and other media into the picture. The use of finger paint, because it cannot be controlled, gives a very direct expression of the inner world which may well be a 'mess' or a 'black splodge' or 'a pooey picture'.

The extract below comes from a chapter entitled 'Art therapy as part of the world of dyslexic children'. The author presents us with a very clear therapeutic setting where there are choices of material, themes and outcome. There is an echo from Lowenfeld's work, discussed in Chapter 1, where the child also needs to repair the damage – that is, to create the perfect or romantic vision, the 'heart's desire' as well as the more painful reality of the traumatic happening.

> We had on offer a range of art materials – clay, paper, paints, scissors, crayons. They could choose their materials and subject matter. I would suggest a theme but this was optional. I was impressed with the intensity and absorption encouraged by the creative process. Sometimes the desired communication was quickly achieved, and its creator wished for some confidential time to share this process. The group was seldom so competitive as to prevent this. Often the individual shared long-buried secrets or faced up to previously inadmissible realities. As the children were away from home, there was a tendency to romanticise their families and their relationship with them. Although very painful, they often revealed the opposite scenario, a more authentic picture of their relationship with their families. (Feilden 1990, p.105)

Story Play

THE EARLY STORY

Children, as we can see, will share their 'world' or story and, often, this will be their experience of the damaging situation which may be in the past or continuing in the present. It is also important for the child to be able to express this story in time – 'has this picture always been like this?'; 'was the picture different a long time ago or before you moved house?' and so on. For many children the 'early story' may have positive memories and this story may help to bring about hope in an otherwise despairing situation.

THE JOURNEY STORY

The 'early story', where it is different, may well lead the child, with the help of the therapist, into the 'journey story' where the child is able to tell the story through pictures, sand, objects, toys, a dolls' house, and so on. The child can thus experience the moves from one state of being to another. This can assist the child not only to 'make sense' of the story but also to have a feeling of 'movement' – that is, that things can move on and change.

In this chapter we have looked at the function of projective play in the normal development of the child and what happens to the child's growth if this does not take place. This included:

- absence of projective play
- rigid projective play
- uncontained projective play.

We considered how projective play could be used in therapeutic intervention, differentiating between play that is exploratory and sensory, manipulative and problem-solving, and that which is symbolic in terms of creating and recreating the child's experience. The next chapter looks at the third developmental stage – that of Role, and how it integrates into the developmental paradigm.

'Grandma, I've got two goldfish and I'm going to call them Rolio and Juniet.' (George, aged 3)

CHAPTER 7

The Playtherapy Method
Role and Dramatic Play

Berowne: All hid, all hid; an old infant play.

(Love's Labours Lost, IV, iii, 78*)*

The third stage of the EPR developmental paradigm, Role, is essential for the child to be able to engage in dramatic play, and it is often the one that therapists find most difficult. If a child is working one to one, then the therapist also has to be 'in-role' which many people find difficult, and non-directive therapists would refuse to do. However, unless children are being seen in groups, the therapy will only stay at the truncated stages of Embodiment and Projection because dramatic play by its very nature needs more than one person.

It may be that the child wants the therapist also in role as was the case with Trevor in Chapter 6. The child may want the therapist as witness and audience, perhaps even performing the function of a chorus and commenting on the play.

Since we organise and construe our world in dramatic form, then it is essential that we can enable a child to progress to the Role stage of EPR. I would suggest that a playtherapist using EPR needs to be a Role sort of person in order to feel comfortable (see Jennings 1998, pp.158–162) or at least to undertake sufficient role play training in order to be adaptable and flexible.

Dramatic play can be said to be at its most fulsome and effective when the therapist and child are both engaged in imaginary characters.

We saw in Chapter 4 how the beginnings of Role are present when a child is born, even though it is expressed physically through Embodiment. The Role stage is the stepping-stone to dramatic play, the important synthesis.

Our roles expand as we relate to the wider world, and we experience both the chance to play roles and the chance to witness them being played by other people.

Dramatic Distancing

If the child chooses an imagined scene or character then we call this 'distanced' from the child's actual experience. The distanced scene will always have connections with the child's own life but it is being enacted through distance. Paradoxically, working through distance usually means we come closer to our own experience.

We will see in the story of Mary that different 'roles' have to be clarified before we proceed. With Mary there is a small amount of distancing as she was asked to become her parents, at least in posture and tone of voice. In Alan's situation (Chapter 4), he was testing out a new aspect of himself – the part of himself that could play; there was no use made of dramatic distancing of himself in a different role until he explored the images of the tractor, then he spoke as the tractor.

If we look back to Chapter 5 in the story of 'The magic forest' there is a dramatisation through roles (or characters) without language – this story is told through movement and sound. There is substantial dramatic distancing as the children take on the characters of either the animals or the trees in the magic forest. In this case the roles become the medium for more social interaction and care and trust as well as the development of the imagination.

Dramatic Play Reality

As children develop they begin to separate the everyday world from the 'let's pretend' world – what I call the two realities. Young children often confuse the two and their play is a mixture of real and imaginary events and actual and pretend people. However, the separation needs to happen more or less by the age of seven, so that a child is aware of the crossover from one to the other. It is possible to see children who are stuck in one or the other.

We should look carefully at how this transition from everyday reality to dramatic play reality is made; it is always a progression from earlier work – either in Embodiment or Projection – which naturally leads into participation in Role.

We must never forget that many children who are not in therapy, do not have the capacity to play – that is, they are non-players.

Horley (1998) surveyed 16 centres which had a total enrolment of 733 four-year-old children in order to look at children who played and those who did not play. She used the following definition of dramatic play:

> ...dramatic play as situation where role playing becomes more complex and includes dressing up, developing dialogue and creating environments within which to play different roles. Scenes and stories are enacted with peers being included although there may be some situations of a child playing in a dramatic way on their own.

One in five children was classed as a non-player of whom 61 per cent were boys. The professional staff used the following words to identify non-players:

- socially immature
- shy
- loner
- runners
- aimless
- aggressive
- uncooperative
- anxious
- perfectionist
- isolated
- withdrawn
- solitary
- disruptive.

We could use many of these words to describe the case history examples in this book. Horley's survey shows that we still need to do more work on 'preventative play' and not just 'curative play'.

Role Models

As well as developing our awareness of others and the roots of a conscience, the importance of playing appropriate role models cannot be over-emphasised. The child with minimal role models is abandoned to a confusing world of impressions with no core identity. All the impressions an infant normally received during the first few weeks, in the way it was cared for, talked to and played with, are absent. It is not surprising that some children have been considered organically damaged as a result of such emotional and social deprivation. We know from the writings on 'wolf' children (Gleitman 1986), that a child takes on the bodily actions and skills of those closest to it. It is important as the child develops that other people, apart from the primary carer, inhabit the child's world in order for an increasing range of role models to be available. The child is thus able to develop more flexibility, and their identity expands.

I am Spiderman and I can jump this fence

Many children have substituted live role models in their social world with an increasing number of media models and characters in stories and soaps. The characters are experienced as real people. This is common in adolescence with media heroes but when media characters are believed to be real people, it is a collapsing of the borders of the everyday world and the imagined or dramatic world.

Absent Role Models

Some children have the resources to survive enormous role deprivation, particularly if they have a well-developed dramatic imagination. Other children become seriously impaired in all areas of their development – physical, emotional, mental and indeed spiritual. Some children cope with an unbearable life through a single role, and this role may become psychotic as the child is unable to deal with the demands of everyday reality. The psychotic role both for children and adults is one where the dramatic reality has taken over the everyday.

Whereas some children are damaged through an absence of role models, others are born into environments where there is a high degree of expectation even before the child is born. Most parents have a notion of their child being the 'dream child' who will live up to their joint fantasies. Most dream baby ambitions become relaxed as the reality of the child becomes more and more a part of the parent's lives.

Rigid Role Models

However, some parents seek to mould a child through the imposition of a set of values and behaviours. This may start from birth with rigid regimes and educational stimulus. For these parents play activity is often restricted to that which can be perceived as 'useful' and 'clean'. Role behaviour is encouraged in order to reproduce adult behaviour, and includes norms and manners that are considered 'acceptable'. Appropriate life and social skills are taught by rote and the parents themselves often have a rigid role relationship with prescribed limits. They will categorise their social world with phrases like 'people like us' and 'people not like us'. The child responds by desperately wanting to conform in order to get affirmation from its parents. However, this rarely happens as the child's efforts are rarely seen as good enough and praise is considered something to be rationed. The child may end up dispirited and depressed and may be further confused if he or she witnesses the behaviour of other adults that does not fall within the prescriptions of the parents.

Although an absence of role model or a rigid role model can have serious implications for children they cannot compare with the damage caused by a role model that is distorted.

Distorted Role Models

I consider a distorted role model to be any behaviour towards a child that is inappropriate to both the age of the child and the relationship with the child. Furthermore it is also a distorted experience for a child to witness inappropriate behaviour in both a relationship and in relation to the child's age. Most distortions are punishable by law although some categories of cruelty are not always easy to identify or prove. Within this range are both the physical and sexual abuse of the child and others in the family. A child may also be a witness or an accomplice to other criminal acts, such as fraud or burglary. As witness, or victim or accomplice, a child is subjected to a situation which he or she is unable to understand. This produces a distortion both of the way the child perceives the world and in the way they experience themselves. Rather than role modelling becoming a positive experience for the appropriate maturation of the child, the distorted role model leads to a chaotic experience of self and other. Because human beings try to resolve chaos and uncertainty we often find that the child adopts a coping mechanism to deal with the distortion.

It is a well-known fact that many victims of child sexual abuse grow up to be perpetrators themselves or continue to be victims in every sexual encounter. Other children may develop *anorexia nervosa* or a similar disorder in an attempt to bring physical control into a situation where there has been a loss of normal control. Victims of violence frequently become violent themselves or continue to find themselves in the role of the receiver of violence. A child who is witness to violent language as the only means of communication may well choose not to speak at all.

Contemporary newspaper accounts of young children being trained to beg, both in England and elsewhere, and of children who are purposely mutilated (the rat children), in order to arouse sympathy and therefore beg more efficiently, demonstrate that the exploitation and abuse of children is still with us. Where any form of inappropriate role modelling, child abuse or destructive child rearing has taken place, the careful application of dramatic playtherapy can be used. One hopes that the opportunity for the child to re-experience a less distorted sense of self, other and the world will encourage a more normal role modelling to take place.

> What it was most impossible to get rid of was the cruel idea that, whatever I had seen, Miles and Flora saw *more* – things terrible and unguessable and that sprang from dreadful passages of intercourse in the past. Such things naturally left on the surface, for the time, a chill which we vociferously denied that we felt; and we had, all three, with repetition, got into such splendid training that we went, each time, almost automatically, to mark the close of the incident, through the very same movements. It was striking of the children, at all events, to kiss me inveterately with a kind of wild irrelevance ... (*The Turn of the Screw,* p.52)

EXAMPLE

Mary was referred for playtherapy as a fourteen-year-old girl suffering from anorexia nervosa. She was a popular girl at school and especially enjoyed all sports and gymnastics. She put a lot of energy and time into these. She trained daily, jogging first thing in the morning and working out in the gym after school. She had received a lot of affirmation for her sports activities and her mother had said in an interview that she thought sports were good for girls as it kept them fit and out of mischief.

It wasn't until she collapsed at a training session that her GP became involved and discovered that Mary weighed five stone (her height was 5 foot 7 inches). It transpired that she had been able to avoid most family meals owing to the preoccupation with sport and had used her dinner money to purchase low-calorie meals. Her parents had been very shocked that their daughter was diagnosed as ill and in need of both physical and psychological treatment.

At her first session, she came in with a beaming smile and asked what I wanted her to do, saying, 'I've never done anything like this before, so you will have to tell me what you want'.

I felt how much easier it would be to fall into her presented role of well-being, smiling and friendly and to take on the role of telling her what to do with her disingenuous innocence. I explained that I had seen the medical reports, that there were concerns about her weight and health, and that it was my job as playtherapist to see if there were any useful areas we could explore together.

She told me that she was fine now. She had just overdone the training a bit and forgotten to eat regularly because she was so busy. She had a very full timetable with sports and school work – but she was OK. I responded by saying that I was not challenging her when she said she felt fine and that she already knew the concern of the doctor and her parents. However, I told her that what did interest me was that she said she felt fine whilst her parents and the doctor thought otherwise. I asked her why she thought there was a difference.

Mary said, 'Everyone is just making a fuss really, just because I overdid it. Mummy and Daddy weren't at all worried. They're terribly pleased at what I'm doing – the sports and so on. They've only become nervy because of what the doctor said, and then the doctor at the hospital.' I then asked, 'So, before you collapsed, neither of your parents were worried about you? They didn't notice that you hadn't been eating?.' She replied that they had always admired how she looked. 'Mummy said how lucky I was not to have puppy fat like she did, and she's quite fat now, you know.' I asked her how she would describe her parents so that I could recognise them. I asked her to help me build a picture. Mary repeated: 'As I said, Mummy is overweight. She could be very attractive – I know she was when she was younger as I have seen pictures of her. She's tallish, black hair and dark eyes; she frowns a lot; she works in a doctor's surgery part-time. Daddy, well, he's tall and very handsome; keeps his figure – he plays squash regularly; he's a solicitor and very brainy and very charming.' I told her that I wasn't sure that I would recognise them. Could she give me more detail? How did they speak; what tone of voice; what did they wear?

This dialogue continued for some time with Mary becoming more confident at describing her parents' roles, or more accurately building up a character profile of each of them, including their clothes. I then went on to ask her to describe herself in the same way. Finally I asked her to choose an animal to represent each of her parents and herself. She said it was impossible. She couldn't see them as animals they were people – so I asked if there were any people in the toys or any story she knew that reminded her of herself and her parents. She immediately said: 'Red Riding Hood – it used to be my favourite story and I played it at junior school. Red Riding Hood is such a pretty little girl; blonde, like me. I always thought Daddy was like the woodcutter who rescued Red Riding Hood.'

It was important not to push the idea of the animals when she obviously resisted; however, I was interested that she did not dismiss it as silly play or as being childish. She said that she could not represent her parents as animals although there were a vast number to choose from. I was left with the question: why was the thought of animals so frightening, threatening? Too near the truth?

It would be so easy to attempt interpretations in this first session when the client has shared such a symbolic fairy story. Has she presented a story she thinks will please the therapist, or a story that she genuinely enjoys; or is she, unconsciously, communicating something less innocent? It could be all of these things and the wrong sorts of questions could break the tentative bridge that has started to be built.

> As we closed the first session, I suggested that she keep a diary of drawings, pictures, poems or stories that she liked or was drawn to, and that she bring it with her to the session next time. Perhaps she could start with Red Riding Hood?
>
> Mary did not attend for the second session and after I had written to her she arrived the following week, smiling and full of apology – she had completely forgotten. Anyway, did she really have to come, as she was so much better and everything was so busy? I reiterated the contract we had agreed of four sessions before we made any decisions about the future. She then went on to say that she hadn't done any of the homework I had set her because she was busy, but she had traced a couple of pictures which she liked from a newspaper. She opened a school exercise book and showed me her tracings of the head of the Pope and a lamb that had been born recently. 'I like them both so much. They are both so ... so pure ... and good. I wish I was like that.' 'Is Red Riding Hood like that?' I asked her. 'She tries to be – oh, she tries so hard to be good and pure, but it's no good,' she replied.
>
> She began to look very distressed at this point and her eyes filled with tears, but she fought them back, put on her smile and said: 'So all she can do is to keep on trying.'.I said: 'It sounds as if she is having to put a great deal of effort into being pure and good.' 'She does, all the time, she can never stop,' said Mary. I asked what would happen if she stopped. Mary replied: 'That would be the end. All the badness would take over and control her. Oh, I know I'm talking about myself as well as Red Riding Hood, but I really cannot say any more.' 'Shall we just talk about Red Riding Hood and her story? How she is now?' I asked. Mary said: 'I'll be OK, but I've some things to tell you and it's such a muddle. No, I will tell you a bit now.' I told her that we only had a very short time now; why didn't she tell me how the muddle felt, or maybe she could draw the muddle instead of using words?

Mary promptly took a black felt pen and drew round and round and round, thought for a moment, placed her two tracings of the Pope and the lamb in the middle, and then said: 'That's how it feels – black and very messy.' Mary asked me to keep the picture for her until the next session and left, saying that she would definitely come and would not forget.

So much speculation is possible on the above disclosure from the story, the two images and then the black drawing. Mary's story that she shared the following week was that some years before, when she was about eleven, her father had confided in her that he had a mistress – a very beautiful woman whom he loved in quite a different way from her mother. He told her that he slept with this woman, and when he was out late and said he was playing squash or going to the club, that was where he was. She expressed a range of emotions as she recounted her story: some delight at being trusted with such a grown-up secret; guilt at her mother not knowing; envy of the woman, and her own attempts to be slim and beautiful like her. She was very confused at being told intimate sexual details by her father and at their being whispered to her in such a conspiratorial way.

She then asked to stay in therapy to try and sort out her feelings, and when she came for her next session said in a partly proud and partly scared voice that her periods had started.

We can see from the above example that Mary undoubtedly had a distorted role-model from her father and probably from her mother as well. It would take many sessions to de-role from the confused roles that Mary had taken on in relation to her identity as a woman and emergent sexual being. Her way of dealing with the conflicts and guilt was to take total control of her body, thereby suppressing her ovulation but also her feelings, and at the same time to emulate the desirable woman her father loved. She had been unable to deal at such an early age with her father's disclosures to her. They in themselves constituted a form of sexual abuse, and also placed an impossible burden on her in relation to her mother. She was unable to cope with the realisation of her fantasy of being so close to her father, and yet in reality she wasn't so close to him, as he had this other woman.

When someone is established as an anorectic it is quite unhelpful to get into a debate about eating habits and exercise unless the person knows that change is crucial and has the necessary motivation. Generally, anorectic people are quite capable of maintaining the role they wish to present and will go to great lengths to avoid detection of destructive behaviour.

It can be helpful to see anorexia as a distorted role and to consider the possible role modelling that has brought it about

Practical Ideas for Role Work

Once a child is ready for role work they will give clear indications by spontaneously taking on a role or requesting to direct a scene, for example. One adolescent said to me 'If you play my mother, I'll be me' (Open University film *Drama with Disturbed Adolescents,* 1972). Children may wish to dramatise a story from a book, a story they have made up or a direct scene from their own lives.

Dramatising a story is different from telling a story and there are important gains for the child when he or she is able to play different elements including the monster. Once a child is able to enact the monster, its power is reduced and fears can be managed more easily.

There are plenty of children's stories which can be used in playtherapy (see Cattanach 1997 for an excellent range). The following monster books are particular favourites of mine:

- *Into the Castle* by June Crebbin
- *The Very Worst Monster* by Pat Hutchins

PROJECTIVE TECHNIQUES AS STARTERS

Most of the techniques described in Chapter 5 can lead into role work. Pictures, scenes, 'worlds', family groupings, and so on, can go beyond the 'illustration' and become 'inhabited' and 'enacted'.

POSTCARDS OF LANDSCAPES

You need a very large collection of picture postcards which include countryside, towns, cities, valleys, mountains, rivers, seas, gardens, woods and forests – fertile as well as barren and stark images. The child chooses one of these to talk about their life and enacts the scenes that take place in the landscape – as people or creatures of various sorts.

POSTCARDS OF PEOPLE

Again, a large collection is needed to provide a spectrum of choices – of different ages, ethnic groups, families, pairs, single people, children of all ages, and so on. In my collection I have many cards from the National Portrait Gallery, London, as well as pictures from the Third World.

Just as Mary, in this chapter, talks about Red Riding Hood, there are many stories with which children readily identify and which they would like to participate in – the following list is a brief résumé of stories that both children and adolescents have asked for:

- The Three Bears
- The Laidley Worm
- Jack and the Beanstalk
- Alice in Wonderland
- The Snow Queen
- The Three Billy Goats Gruff
- The Three Little Pigs
- Beauty and the Beast

These stories may be told and enacted during the telling, or enacted after the telling; the endings may be changed if the child so wishes. Different roles may be experienced so that the child expands his or her own perception and role repertoire.

This chapter has been concerned with the third stage of the EPR paradigm: Role. We have considered the issue of children who do not play as well as the crucial question of role modelling.

'I had this skin when I was born didn't I? I had *my* skin before George.'
(Harry, aged four)

CHAPTER 8

Playtherapy Applications

Bastard: According to the fair play of the world
Let me have audience.

(King John, V, ii, 118)

We have now established the basis of the Playtherapy Method: Embodiment, Projection and Role which can be used to structure any playtherapy or dramatherapy session. Indeed I have widened the application of EPR to ordinary drama workshops and the training of actors and directors (Jennings 1999, in preparation).

In this chapter we will consider the thinking through that is necessary before practice in order for playtherapists to feel sufficiently supported and guided on the one hand and to feel confident enough for some risk-taking on the other. In both this chapter and the following one, we are really addressing the playtherapist's ritual/risk factor.

The previous chapters have considered the various developmental contexts for this work, looked at a wide range of methods and their application. As has been said earlier, the Playtherapy Method is a multi-model intervention which takes as its basis the dramatic nature of both human beings and play activity. However, we need to consider the reality of its application and what actually happens when a child comes into the room – what do we open our mouths and say, if anything at all?

Referral for Playtherapy

Referral for playtherapy can arise from a carefully assessed situation that involves the professional team from social services, health, education and probation, or from a haphazard response hoping to 'do something'. The result of this latter initiative takes the form of the playtherapist being asked, 'would you just ...'. Regrettably, there are times when it is felt necessary to be *seen* to do something – especially in relation to children – rather than first to think through an appropriate plan of action. It is to be hoped that the implementation of the Children Act 1991 will influence these less acceptable procedures and involve families as a whole and not just the damaged children from those families.

When considering the application of the Playtherapy Method, it is most important that appropriate assessment and referral be made. It also makes a measurable difference to the outcome of the therapy if the family has been involved as much as possible. The playtherapist is not a substitute parent for the child, even though the playtherapy itself may facilitate some re-parenting. It is important for the child who continues to live at home not to feel a divided parental loyalty.

In fostering and adoption too, it is important for the natural parents to have a place in the child's world. Too often in the past, attempts have been made to make the child 'forget' and make a new start in a new home, with new adults and new possessions; yet it is so often the old and worn toy that is the 'treasure'. Renée's poem incorporated her birth family during the process of adoption preparation.

Renée's Poem

The Pond

The pond is yellow
Yellow like the sun
It's pretty and I love it
Lesley lives in the pond with mum
They live on the bottom of the pond
No one lives with them.

The pond is in Lordship Lane
They are happy – they live in a pink sea shell.

Renée's (aged 8) accompanying picture drawn in gold pen showed the yellow pond and the new house she would be living in. The house is drawn in quite a fragmented way with doors and windows as separate items.

Outlining the Playtherapy Process

Once assessment is complete (a process carried out with the family if possible), it is important that any decisions are explained (usually more than once) to all those concerned. Parents and other family members need to have playtherapy explained to them as much as the child does; families need to understand that the child's behaviour may well deteriorate in the initial stages. Parents need to be reassured that the confidentiality of the therapy need not threaten them – that much of what the child communicates is private (just as all people need privacy) – and that the child will tell them things when he or she is willing and ready. If this is not made clear, many parents (and teachers too) will cross-examine children about what they have done and said in the session – and it can then be ridiculed or criticised. Most parents feel very guilty about the fact that their child needs therapy and ask the question 'Where did I go wrong?'. They may resent what they may regard as the miracles that happen within a short space of time or even sabotage the sessions by arriving late, or cancelling them or undermining the playtherapist's relationship with the child in some other way.

It may be that, during the time of the child's playtherapy, support can also be arranged for the parents – and indeed other members of the family – and, where family therapy resources are available, sessions for the family as a whole. While fundamental change can be brought about by working with the whole family, this does not necessarily exclude work with an individual as well. There is not scope here to debate properly the theory and practice of family therapy – whether systemic or strategic – except to suggest that the family therapist's belief in work in the here and now with the family as a whole represents a major breakthrough in the assumptions we make about therapy. The family therapist does not focus on the presenting patient, that is, the person labelled as having the problem, but with the family as a whole, seeing the family as an interlocking system which has become dysfunctional. As is often the case, one member of the family can take on the problems on behalf of the family as a whole.

As an example of how an untreated family can manifest its dysfunction through taking it in turns to be seriously ill, we can look at the Parkin family.

This family claimed they were ordinary, traditional and law-abiding. Mr Parkin owned a small grocery and general store with a sub-post office on the outskirts of a small country town. Mrs Parkin ran the house and occasionally helped her husband. Margaret, Robert and Anne were born within two or three years of each other. The family came to the attention of the GP when Mrs Parkin took her daughter Anne to the surgery on several occasions because she was 'poorly', 'sickly' or 'not eating'. At the same time, her mother would say to the GP, 'of course, I was like that as a child – I did not eat – I was thin – I missed school a lot – I was ill …'

Margaret left home as soon as possible, having been the 'hard worker' at school. She promptly joined the Women's Royal Army Corps and applied to work overseas; she visited home once or twice a year when she was on leave.

Anne continued to have time off from school as well as invalid foods, tonics and vitamins bought by her mother. This continued for several years – although teachers had suggested that Anne might be anorexic – until she disappeared one day and was found sitting on a park bench, looking withdrawn and possibly in a psychotic state. She was admitted to hospital and given anti-depressants and a brief period of psychotherapy before being discharged and recommended to attend a day centre. She found a home in a half-way hostel, attended the day centre for some months, and had regular check-ups because she and her mother were both convinced that she had an organic problem. However, she did not wish to return to her family home and continued to live in the hostel for a couple of years. She was still unwell, and found increasing difficulty in dealing with the imposed rules of the hostel.

Meanwhile the parents continued as before and their son Robert left school and started working in the shop and post office with his father. Of her own accord, Anne made a decision to leave the hostel and live in a bed-sit on her own. In less than a month, Robert had a psychotic breakdown and was sectioned and admitted to hospital. The recommendation came that he should leave home and live in a half-way hostel (he was still on medication) which he refused to do and went back home again. In a matter of weeks his mother developed a stomach ulcer which allegedly did not respond to treatment. Thus the role of 'patient' moved from daughter to son to mother. The family refused any type of intervention, believing that the only problems were physical ones. Robert still behaves strangely from time to time, something which usually precipitates a deterioration of Mrs Parkin's condition. Neither parent has any intention of encouraging Robert to leave home and sees it as his right to stay with them if he so chooses. The sisters Margaret and Anne survive by staying right away from the family.

The above example is an obvious illustration of a family which maintains its dysfunction by not allowing any disruption of the status quo. Although we might use psychoanalytic theory to offer explanations in the case of this family – such as, for example, the unresolved Oedipal conflicts of Robert –

we would be impelled to suggest that all the family members would need therapy of some kind. Notice how the father is strangely absent in the above scenario. In reality he *is* absent to his family because he is always busy checking stock and adding up figures and is never around to be talked to or with. If the family were motivated to come for therapy then it would seem that here-and-now intervention with a systemic family therapist might well allow change.

In the above hypothesis, however, the family has to be both motivated and willing for change to take place. Very often therapists have to work with a child in need, without the co-operation or more extended involvement of the family. Playtherapy intervention with the whole family is discussed later in this chapter.

Diagnosis Through Playtherapy

It is often hoped that playtherapy will yield information that can be used to diagnose the various problems that children manifest. Some agencies see the function of playtherapy as being that very thing – diagnostic and disclosure work. This comes about from various needs, the obvious one of course being that for evidence that will stand up in a court of law, and many child abuse cases have not proceeded because children have been unable to testify, especially when they have had to face the perpetrator in an open court.

Although currently there appears to be a change in the way such cases are conducted, nevertheless there is still a preoccupation with the facts. The child is seen as a locked box and the therapist is expected to find the key. The roles of the therapist in terms of disclosure and therapy *must* be separated if there is to be satisfactory healing intervention.

Furthermore, if a child appears grossly disturbed or damaged, then diagnostic interviews and assessment are necessary if the most appropriate form of therapy is to take place. This takes place before the playtherapy or other intervention commences.

Usually a child psychologist and/or psychiatrist is involved in the primary diagnostic period (together with reports from others who have been involved such as social workers and teachers). Clinicians state that formal diagnosis of childhood disorder should rely on standardised, reliable clinical criteria. There are a number of standard tests which the reader may refer to in psychology texts. These texts usually classify childhood disorders under the following headings: developmental; behavioural; emotional; habit; learning difficulties. Of course not all theorists agree on what should come under each of the headings (for example, is anorexia nervosa classified as an emotional problem or a faulty habit?) and, therefore, on the best method of intervention!

It is not within the scope of this book to enter the debate which surrounds many of these issues – not least the nature/nurture and the behavioural therapy/psychodynamic therapy perennial. Some of them are illustrated in Chapter 2. We need to acknowledge that playtherapists may have an orientation within only one model (such as object relations or behaviourist for example) or a variety of models (often termed the eclectic or multi-model) in relation to clinical theory.

However, the question that concerns us here is whether playtherapy methods can be used for diagnosis.

Behar and Rapaport (1983) say that play observation may be a useful *adjunct* in some circumstances, such as when:

1.   Contradictions or doubtful assertions are found in the reports of parents and teachers

2.   A discrepancy is sensed between reports and clinical observation

3.   The child is too young mentally to be interviewed verbally or, for a variety of reasons, the verbal communications are suspect

4.   The child is too shy or too withdrawn to be otherwise engaged.

However, they also refer to 'the clinical, intuitive, hypothesis generating process which play interview provides'. This is similar to what Peter Brook calls 'the formless hunch' (Brook 1988, p.155). Clinician and theatre artist alike are prepared to acknowledge that there is a non-quantifiable area of human observation based on 'gut reaction'. Gut reaction plays a large part in the way we both assess and practise as artistic therapists of various kinds, especially in playtherapy when we may be working with children who are pre-verbal or non-verbal.

This intuitive 'hunch' may well be an indicator for therapeutic exploration but must not be confused with the therapist's interpretations and explanations of the child's play. However I would suggest that the 'hunch' is likely to be of use in the early playtherapy sessions when determining which direction to take; as the previous case histories illustrate, in diagnostic work interviews the intuitive impressions contribute to the overall picture.

In the next section we shall look at the several playtherapy assessment sessions that are usually necessary before a programme can begin.

Playtherapy Assessment

When a child has been referred for playtherapy, it is necessary first to have several playtherapy assessment sessions. These enable the therapist *and* the child to 'take stock'. Decisions need to be made about the optimum number of sessions (three or four? Over a period of six weeks? Over three, six, nine, twelve months? How often? Weekly? Fortnightly?). The following are some questions that need to be asked during the first and second sessions.

- What does the child want from the therapy?
- What does the therapist want from the therapy?
- Does the child actually understand what playtherapy is?
- What materials in the playtherapy room draw the child?
- Where does the child respond on the Embodiment–Projection–Role (EPR) paradigm?
- How does the child respond on the ritual/risk (R/R) scale?

Many people may feel, like Oaklander and others, that the therapist can start from where the child is and then see what happens.

> My goal is to help the child become aware of herself and her existence in her world.

and

> The process I present is self-monitoring, I believe there is no way you can make a mistake if you have good will and refrain from interpretation and judgements – if you accept the child with respect and regard.

and

> I never force a child to do or say something he absolutely does not want to do or say. I try to avoid interpretations, so I check out my own guesses and hunches with the child. If he's not interested in responding, that's fine. I don't insist that he 'own' anything if he needs to keep things safely protected. (Oaklander 1978, pp.62–63)

Virginia Axline (1947/1969) puts forward her non-directive approach:

> Non-directive play therapy, as we have said before may be described as an opportunity that is offered to the child to experience growth under the most favorable conditions. Since play is his natural medium for self-expression, the child is given the opportunity to play out his accumulated feelings of tension, frustration, insecurity, aggression, fear, bewilderment, confusion. (p.16)

and

> Because primary emphasis is placed upon the active participation of the
> self in this growth experience, the term non-directive seems inadequate.
> While this term does accurately describe the role of the counsellor, in that
> he maintains sufficient self-discipline to restrain any impulses which he
> might have to take over the client's responsibility it is certainly inaccurate
> when applied to the role of the client. Instead, self-directive therapy
> seems to be a more accurate and more honestly descriptive term.

Margaret Lowenfeld (1935) goes as far as to state that the true observation of
children at play is impossible because it means the presence of an adult. At
her Institute of Child Psychology, an out-patient clinic for the treatment and
study of children, she conducted a programme twice weekly for children
with a variety of problems, including: emotional disturbance; chronic
disorders such as epilepsy, asthma, catarrh, debility, constipation, enuresis;
children who were unable to adjust themselves socially; and children with
educational difficulties. An intelligence test was given by a worker, with
whom the child was unfamiliar, to every child before its entry to the
playroom.

Lowenfeld was very strict about the playrooms being only for the
children and the therapists – parents were not allowed in; and therapists had
to work at the same physical level as the child. However she was also
concerned that the therapist's scale of values is different from the scale of
values of the child – and that the difference is so radical that the adult can only
be experienced as judgemental or criticising.

Smilansky's (1968) six evaluating factors (see Chapter 2) can be used in
assessment. These categories are very useful in a diagnostic period when
considering the direction in which the playtherapy needs to go. However, the
above categories fall under the third stage of EPR since they start with the
capacity to role play. They would be more useful for the Playtherapy Method
as part of a wider conceptual framework.

Eleanor Irwin (1983) describes how she uses dramatic play materials to
stimulate fantasy and play in several methods in diagnosis and treatment. She
says:

> Each offers an opportunity to observe the child's verbal and non-verbal
> responses; the thinking and decision making process; the response to and
> the use of materials; the process, form, and content of the play; and the
> child's interaction with the therapist.

and

> Experience has indicated that a variety of diagnostic approaches are
> helpful, as each gives data about different aspects of personality
> functioning. In addition, variety allows for the child's idiosyncratic
> responses to materials and media and gives the adult a chance to learn
> about natural interests and experiences.

The several playtherapy orientations described above all emphasise the
importance of play in diagnosis and assessment but demonstrate a very wide
spectrum of approaches, which range from 'the way in and follow the child'
to the more 'interpretive and psychoanalytic view'.

Embodiment, Projection and Role in Diagnosis and Assessment

In the previous chapters, EPR as a developmental way of working is
described with a variety of methods for application in the playtherapy setting
both with children and adolescents. Having described the component parts
of each of the stages and the broad ages at which they will occur, we are now
in a position to consider EPR in relation to diagnosis and assessment.

We must remember that any chart or form for recording our work is as
good as the categories on the chart and I would recommend that
playtherapists evolve and experiment with their own charts.

The following structure may help the playtherapist to pace their
interventions, to be able to get into the child's rhythm. This becomes a
structure within which the child meets the therapist, and the stages do not
follow in a straight line. Earlier stages are returned to and worked with in
different ways, and EPR will occur at each stage.

Pre-session: the child is referred and clinical information (if appropriate)
is available.

Name: _Kete_		Dramatherapist/Playtherapist: _Rw._		
DOB ___ **Session** **Aged** _9_ **Date**	**1** _1_	**2** _2_	**3**	**Recommendations**
EMBODIMENT:		_Initiated contact_		
1. Touch, Eye-contact	_guarded eye contact_	_Pleased to see me_	_Drawn + tense_	_Work on self_
2. Spatial Awareness	_Sat at table_	_Sat at table/MAT_	_MAT /Table_	_Image important_
3. Working With/Against				
4. Whole Body		_eager to help bring toys in_	_Sad_	
5. Body Parts				
6. Body Self/Image	_poor_		_poor_	
7. Mimicry/Innovation				
8. Other				
PROJECTION				
1. Sand/Sand and Water				_Well engaged_
2. Clay/Plasticine		_-_		_loves the cloths to enstore_
3. Pencil/Crayons	_✓_	_✓_	_✓_	_+ creating stories_
4. Paint (finger/brush)		_/_	_/_	_1. Dolls_ _2. furniture_
5. Single Image/Whole Picture	_✓_			_3. Glitter Pens gold/silver_
6. Single/Large Toys				
7. Environmental*		_dolls + doll furniture_	_dolls + doll furn_	
8. Other	_puppets_			
ROLE				
1. Body Movement/Gesture	_Suspicious_		_Sad/tense_	_Role work v._
2. Sound/Speech	_ARTICULATE_		_quiet._	_Dolls_
3. Mimicry/Innovation	_–_	_Innovation -story_	_Innovation - story_	_stories without hope - bleak_
4. Brief/Sustained		_✓_	_✓_	
5. Relationship with another role	_–_		_.._	
6. Role Development	_–_	_STORY - uses dolls_	_STORY u/e Dolls_	
7. Development Scene/Situation				
8. Other		_nuce - Deprivation_		_STORY - Print dead_

GENERAL OBSERVATIONS

Stories are bleak - without hope - need to introduce some hope -
Also stories reflect her being adrift between situations - life is not predictable
- may find Dramatic play positive in future .

* houses/jungles ,etc., with boxes and material.

Figure 8.1 Embodiment – Projection – Role Observation Chart

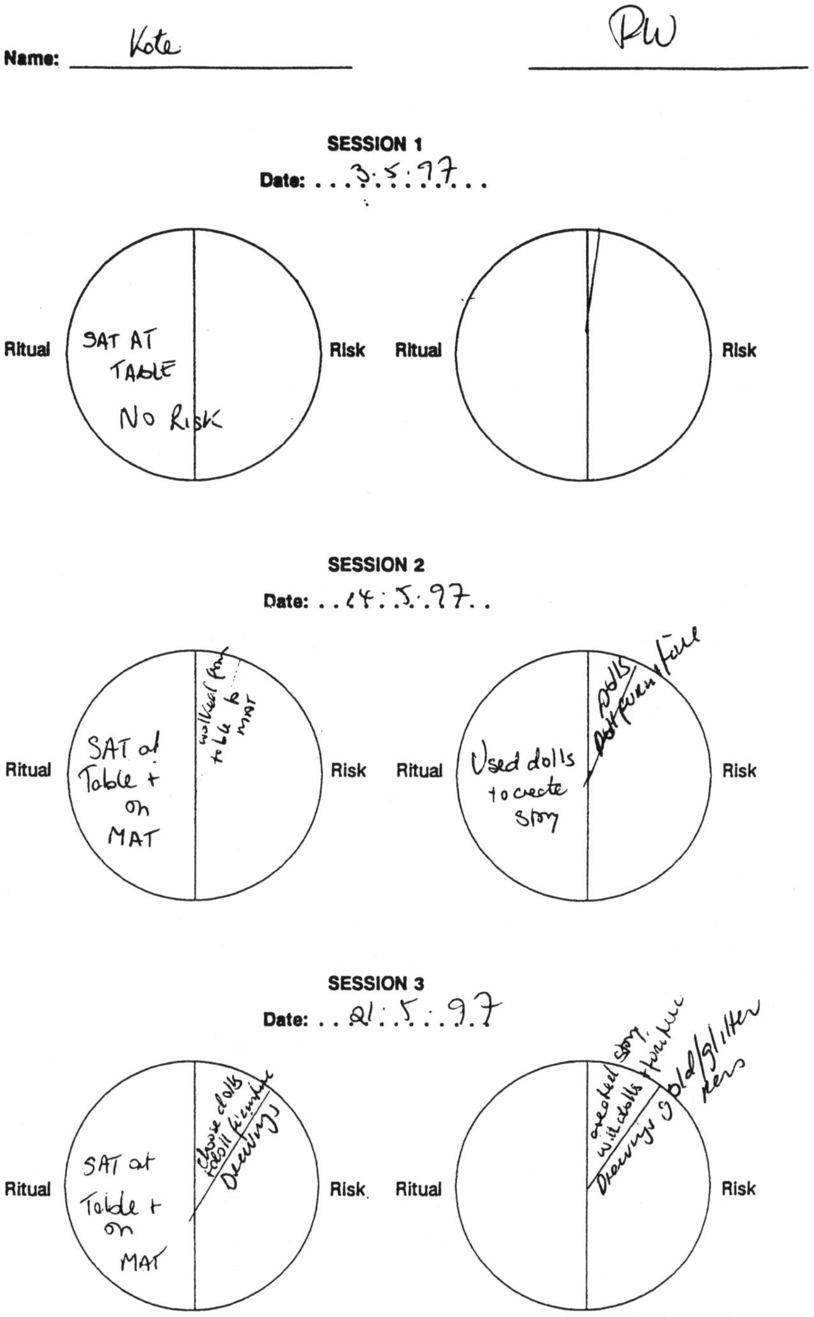

Name: _Kate_   _PW_

SESSION 1
Date: ...3.5.97...

Ritual | SAT AT TABLE   No Risk | Risk   Ritual | | Risk

SESSION 2
Date: ..14.5.97..

Ritual | SAT at Table + on MAT   walked from table to MAT | Risk   Ritual | Used dolls to create story   Dolls not even feel | Risk

SESSION 3
Date: ..21.5.97

Ritual | SAT at Table + on MAT   chose dolls doll furniture Drawings | Risk   Ritual | created story with dolls furniture Drawing gold/glitter pens | Risk

Figure 8.2 Ritual / Risk Observation Chart

Stage 1: Warm-Up

1. *Meeting the child:* establishing roles and relationships; establishing the framework and ground rules (questions/explanations, etc.)

2. *Random play:* diagnostic/assessment sessions: use of EPR, risk/ritual observation, BASIC Ph, 6PSM.

N.B. Supervision and planning are particularly important during this stage. (A lot of checking out during this time; further questions and testing by child.)

Stage 2: Development: Engagement and Interaction

3. *Basic trust:* some risk-taking with self and other; some sharing but also testing

4. *Basic interaction:* therapist figures more in the play; dramatic relationship is beginning

5. *Developed dramatic play:* awareness of sub-texts; greater risk-taking

6. *Therapist as actor:* when the child delegates 'risky' roles

7. *Therapist as audience:* important for witnessing what the child needs to be witnessed

8. *Therapist as co-actor:* therapist participates with the child's direction in the dramatic scene; deeper engagement.

Stage 3: Closure: Re-working and Reflection

9. *Post-dramatic play:* therapist and child are able to reflect on the drama

10. *Re-working scenes:* the child is able to re-direct scenes and explore different outcomes

11. *Integration of experience:* the child can view the drama as a whole and recognise self in drama and drama in self

12. *Closure and lights up:* working toward the ending and walking away from the drama and the relationship.

It will be helpful for the playtherapist if his or her relationship with the child is a dramatic one; that he or she is engaged through role and character for the duration of the dramatic play and may therefore be flexible according to the child's needs.

It will be clear from the above structure that the child can develop a deeper engagement and interaction through the play and therefore deeper disclosure may happen usually at a symbolic level. The playtherapist must be especially vigilant at this point and not change the frame of reference.

Any exploration must be done within the play and not through the goal posts being moved.

If we make shifts once our basic frame of reference has been established, a child will become confused and may become even more insecure than when they started.

As part of a contract with a child who is coming into playtherapy, there must be some idea of duration. We need to remember that a child's memory has a limited span and often open-ended playtherapy can produce gross dependence and a lot of insecurity. The Playtherapy Method, because it mobilises many resources in a child from the beginning, is usually used for short and medium-term therapy, though the method is still appropriate for longer-term work when necessary. I prefer to have a series of contracts negotiated with the child, which can then be reviewed if either the therapist or the child requests it. For example, a period of three diagnostic sessions followed by a contract for six further sessions (Stages 2 and 3 in the chart) is a reasonable short-term agreement that a child can readily grasp. Further lengths of time can be negotiated as required and if there are resources, then a longer-term arrangement, say two to six months can follow. However, if there is no more time available, a child must know that clearly at the outset.

This chapter has dealt with issues of referral and assessment for playtherapy and includes methods for structuring sessions. Above all, it emphasises the continuing dialogue with the child and the need for honesty and integrity.

'Do people die to make room for babies to be born? If so, who died to make room for Alfie?' (Harry, aged four)

CHAPTER 9

Playtherapy in Practice

Gloucester. You are my guests. Do me no foul play, friends.

(King Lear, III, vii, 31*)*

Nothing can be more daunting for the playtherapist who has reached the point in a book such as this, where all sorts of ideas are described and case histories given, than to go and practise. Other people's ideas and techniques are all very well, but we do not feel comfortable with them until we have made them our own. It is important during training for playtherapists to try and test out the different ideas on each other, friends and the children of friends.

Many people react with dismay when they experiment with a new method, only to find that the responses are different from those that they expected. Many people ask, 'What is the first thing you say when you actually enter the playtherapy room? How do you deal with the child who does nothing? What happens when a child does "not engage"?' When this happens it is easy to slip into interpretations about the child, which is often I think a device for reducing therapist's anxiety, rather than looking at the way we actually present ourselves and our methods to children and considering whether they may be clearer, or more confident, or more flexible, for example.

Furthermore, applying a technique that somebody else has described, so that it is like a recipe, just does not work. We need to make a technique our own and find our own way of doing it, before we actually apply it in the playtherapy setting. People will say 'I don't feel comfortable doing this or that method', and my reply is 'then just don't do it. If you don't feel comfortable the child certainly won't'. Though it is useful to find out why we do not feel comfortable, without it becoming a guilt trip.

This book describes the application and the underlying theory of the Playtherapy Method, which can be integrated with any other approach without a conflict of ideas. However it can also be applied in its own right and many people will have had a basic training in a Playtherapy Method on their courses. The advantage of the Playtherapy Method is that it is flexible in approach, can be used diagnostically or as therapy and can be adapted to any space where playtherapy is taking place.

I spoke earlier about the rhythm of playtherapy and this just takes time for the newly trained therapist to tune into. Detailed recording of each session and the guidance of an experienced supervisor will assist this process. The following recording sheet can be used to organise our descriptions of and reflections on the session (see Figure 9.1).

You will notice that I have included on the recording sheet the 'therapist's reflections' before the session. It is important to trust our gut reaction and I want to emphasise the importance of the creativity and imagination of the playtherapist in relation to the child. You will be left with a host of impressions before and after the session and the temptation is to tie it all up in meaningful explanations. Once you have recorded the session, and that may well take as long as the session itself, especially in the early stages of practice, allow the material to 'free float' for a while and scan your own reactions and associations as to what went on in the session. The golden rule is 'don't try and force order on what might seem chaotic'; or *stay with the chaos and the meaning will emerge.*

Personal Anecdote

The following are diary notes during some client work quoted in Jennings (1990, pp.79, 80), when I became stuck and also had physical pain and anxiety about the borders.

> I am aware of feeling heavy, the shoulder pain continues together with a feeling of something being just over the horizon – that I ought to be aware of. OUGHT? Am I stuck too in expectation? I look at the photo again and realise that I have not fully de-roled myself (an occupational hazard for dramatherapists), and in a busy week of teaching, writing and working with clients, I make a conscious decision to have time for a complete change.
>
> I take a couple of hours off for a walk on Hampstead Heath – to scuff leaves in the autumn chill and spend time by the ponds – few people are there on a midweek afternoon and the wind bites sharply – I start to run,

BRIEF RECORDING OF PLAYTHERAPY SESSION

Child's Name _____   Playtherapist _____

Session Number _____   Date _____

Therapist's reflections before session:

Possible media and themes:

Mood/atmosphere at beginning: child

                                                 therapist

Description of actual media and methods used:

E

P

R

Description of content expressed through above:

Graph of levels of engagement throughout the session:

Mood/atmosphere at closure: child

                                               therapist

Thoughts on the session: the child

                                               the dramatic play

                                               the self

Any action which needs to be taken?

Thoughts for the next session:

Figure 9.1 Brief Recording of Playtherapy Session Sheet

shouting into the wind and end up gasping for breath, leaning against a tree trunk – the pools are still with ripple movements on the surface as the wind blows in intermittent gusts – there are two or three fishermen, still and silent under their green umbrellas – I keep walking and decide to circuit the pools.

Tramp, tramp, leaves and mud – face dry from the wind – time will soon be up – the sound of voices blows across and I turn to put the hair out of my eyes – there are two children coming closer with an adult woman – the children are holding hands and approach the water – the boy is pointing out a half sunken tree in the centre of the pool – 'Look, it's a monster from the deep', he says, and his sister (I assume) opens her eyes wide and starts to suck her thumb – the adult woman, who looks bored and disinterested, shakes them both and gestures them to walk on – she walks away, frozen faced – the children stay by the pool and they hold on to each other – I'm just watching, half concealed by a tree – it feels very familiar and I'm riveted – the children are staring at the sunken tree and the dark water lapping round the submerged trunk – there is a tangle of leaves, twigs and feathers caught up in the branches – just then a loud voice breaks the silence:

COME HERE – NOW!

The children start, look at each other, and walk meekly in the direction of the voice of their companion – the scene returns to its quietness, the wind and water cover over the little interlude that I have witnessed – I am left feeling uneasy.

I start to walk away – then the image hammers onto my brain – *The Turn of the Screw* – Henry James – that's the image that has eluded me from the group – the children – frozen – a sense of evil –

I transferred my eyes straight to little Flora, who, at the moment, was about ten yards away. My heart had stood still for an instant with the wonder and terror of the question whether she too would see; and I held by breath while I waited for what a cry from her, what some sudden innocent sign either of interest or alarm, would tell me. I waited, but nothing came; then, in the first place – and there is something more dire in this, I feel, than in anything I have to relate – I was determined by a sense that within a minute all spontaneous sounds from her had dropped; and in the second by the circumstance that also within the minute she had, in her play, turned her back to the water. This was her attitude when I at last looked at her – looked with the confirmed conviction that we were still, together, under direct personal notice. She had picked up a small flat piece of wood which happened to have in it a little hole that had evidently suggested to her the idea of sticking in another fragment that might figure as a mast and make the thing a boat. (*The Turn of the Screw*, p.181)

I walk home with a lighter step – I don't address the image – this is my two hour break so I put it on the back-burner for future attention.

When we are scanning or 'free floating' or even dreaming about things that are relevant to our client work, we need to check out whether this material belongs more to us than to the clients we are working with.

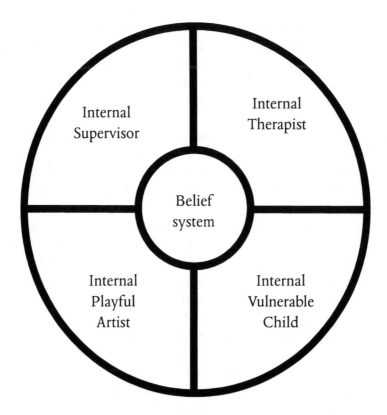

Figure 9.2 Mandala chart for playtherapists to complete about themselves (you can also adapt it for use with children: 'Things I'm good at', 'Things I'm scared of', 'Things I play at', 'who guides me', etc.).

The Mandala Method, (Jennings (1998, 1999, in press) which helps to integrate role function, is very useful for the playtherapist to record from time to time.

The above diagram, although simplistic, gives the four main areas of our internal states together with our belief system and by using this as a large chart that we can write things on and colour, we can be helped to understand our own roles and processes. Our internal therapist is that part of ourselves that is professionally trained and informs us how to work. Our internal vulnerable child may be naughty, or shy, or creative, or good, but it is that side of ourselves that makes the necessary connection with the child. This connection is then informed in terms of 'how to proceed' by the skills of the internal therapist. The internal supervisor may feel like a critical judge but needs to be developed as a benign support to assist you if you are stuck or to challenge your judgement if you are feeling ambivalent. The more we have good supervision the more we develop our own internal supervisor. Our internal playful artist is always there as our creative and artistic self that can both create in its own right and stimulate other areas. Sometimes we lose sight of our internal artist, just as our clients do and it is important to rediscover our own playful potential, which can sustain not only our playtherapy practice but also our everyday life. Our belief system is connected to all the internal states and may be a formal religious or philosophical system, or may be our own code of ethics for life and work. Our sense of right and wrong, our concern for humanity, which are within this core belief system, have all been influenced by the play of our own childhood.

The Mandala Method can also be used both with adults and children as part of the therapeutic process or as a diagnostic intervention. Everybody has an internal guide, internalised skills, an internal creative artist and a vulnerable aspect of themselves with is underpinned by a belief system. When a person comes into therapy the 'vulnerable' segment has usually grown out of proportion to the rest and a person may feel de-skilled, lost and non-creative, feelings which may be accompanied by disillusionment about their beliefs. If we adapted the Mandala to work with children we could call the different sections the things we feel good at (skills), the things we don't feel good about (vulnerability), the things we like playing (artist), and our ideas about why we do what we do (guide). Whether child or adult, the belief system can be destroyed if the person has experienced severe trauma. By taking a view through the Mandala of a person it can help us to address all aspects of our clients, rather than just the vulnerable side which may be what is initially presented to us. Too often professional carers and therapists view people as a collection of problems rather than seeing the problems as issues within a wider context. By working with people's strengths rather than just with their perceived weaknesses we can establish a way of working that focuses on health, rather than just addressing well-being.

The following are some areas that I find many playtherapists find difficult in application. None is greater than the area of child abuse, as more and more incidents of abuse of all kinds are being reported and roles and relationships are being constantly redefined. The hapless child can become a victim of the system and not just of the abuse itself, as there are tidal waves of accusation and counter-accusation. It is important for the playtherapist to remember that it is not appropriate for them both to diagnose and treat a victim of child abuse, whether the abuse is physical, or sexual, or emotional. If the playtherapist is working diagnostically, then this will be part of a range of assessments that are made prior to treatment and the child needs to know that any information gleaned is not necessarily confidential. The playtherapist will be part of a team, and may even be the person who presents evidence in court, if court proceedings are involved. Evidence that is gleaned from symbolic play is usually not considered sufficient evidence for court cases.

I am not a playtherapist who advocates diagnostic work using anatomically explicit dolls; both play and reality converge in these dolls and the fact that children may play in sexually explicit ways is not necessarily a sign of sexual abuse. The child may well, through BASICPh or 6PSM, be able to communicate stories of their abuse, but as diagnostic assessment for *evidence*, this would need to be tested both in and out of the play reality.

When playtherapy is used for the treatment of the child, the focus is different. There is less pressure on 'disclosure work' and on testing whether or not we think something is *true*. We start from the premise that everything the child tells us is true – *at some level* – and it becomes apparent during the therapy which these levels are, how much needs to be explicit and how much can stay within the symbolism of the play.

> However hurt the child – healing metaphors facilitate the process of recovery (Lahad, personal communication 1999)

However distressing we may find the child's situation, the most important quality we can give the child is that of belief. It is appropriate that the child knows that we can feel sorrow, anger and pain through our empathy (not our sympathy) – as long as it is the child's pain we are sharing and we are not superimposing our own.

It should be remembered that even when a child has been severely abused and this has necessitated the child being taken to a place of safety and the abuser being placed in custody, if a parent or sibling is involved, the child will need to work through many ambivalent feelings. However angry the child may feel, he or she also needs to express love and grief and the loss of people and places. Often the child is unable to express the anger since so many of his or her own feelings are confused in relation to the abuse (Cattanach 1992), and many children blame themselves, especially when mothers have told daughters that it is their fault that their fathers abused them. The healing metaphor in the playtherapy needs to allow the child to express the multiple feelings towards the abuser and the abuse.

In her excellent book *Play Therapy with Abused Children* (1993), Ann Cattanach describes very poignantly the way children feel when they have been abused. The children are able to articulate through the playtherapy such thoughts as, 'Don't do that to my grand-daughter. The babies' granddad did it. Poor babes'. This illustrates how children can be articulate about their experiences through the medium of the playtherapy.

If disclosure happens during the course of therapy, then the play-therapist's supervisor will be able to advise on the best course of action. Most codes of ethics and practice acknowledge the fact that confidentiality can be broken if there is a danger to clients or other people.

The following case history illustrates how a playtherapist had to select which area of a child's experience might be helpful to work with.

> Shaun was referred for playtherapy at the age of eight, after he had been taken into care, because of incestuous abuse by an uncle. He was awaiting a long-term foster family. He was staying in a children's home with a large number of 'mixed' children who were variously 'in transit'. Shaun had precipitated a referral for therapy by persistently scarring himself on his arms with sharp metal objects. His psychiatric assessment had shown no severe mental health problem and the observation was that this was a child who was still in shock.
>
> At the first session Shaun sat mute, twiddling with a button and occasionally picking up something and putting it down in a desultory way. He rarely looked at the playtherapist but gazed towards the window and the door.

The playtherapist is having to select which area of this plethora of experience might be helpful for Shaun – especially as he is not yet in a permanent place of safety. Note how she presents that selection to the child, an intuitive hunch that seems to pay off.

> The playtherapist says to Shaun, 'Shaun, it is your choice what you do here in the play room – I am here to help if you want – however, there is something I want to say first – I know you have had a very scary time in your family and you must be worried about what is happening to everyone'. (A glimmer of recognition from Shaun.) The therapist continues, 'I know you are also living in a temporary place where you aren't happy while various decisions are being made about the future – everything must feel very confusing – and nothing can be sorted out in a hurry – maybe we could concentrate on what feels the most important thing right now – such as the place where you are living now'. (Shaun looks directly at the therapist and then looks down, his eyes full with tears.) 'I hate it, I hate it,' he mutters under his breath.

(The naïve therapist would perhaps want to find out what he hated – or might pre-suppose that it was only the incest he was talking about.)

> Shaun says, ' … there are four children in my room and one of them wets and it smells – and I sat on it once by mistake – and then I smelt'.

(Again, is this a metaphor? It may well be but also Shaun is describing something that has actually happened and that is causing him great distress.)

> The therapist asks, 'Could you draw a picture of where you live at the moment?' Shaun replies, 'No – I can't – if I draw it then it means it will be real and I don't want it to be real'. The therapist says, 'We both know it will be real for a short time but not for a long time'. Shaun says, 'What is a short time? A few days?' The therapist replies, 'We can find out how long it is likely to be – but it will be several weeks not days'. Shaun then asks, 'Weeks not months? Not days but weeks? Lots of weeks? Can I just draw?'

Notice how eloquent Shaun is when he says, 'Can I just draw?' The home was something that he needed to talk about and the therapist was able to respond to him needing just to be in the now while these enormous changes were going on around him. The therapist and Shaun were able to negotiate a contract of four sessions where he could say and do whatever he felt like doing.

Shaun later says, 'when the big things happen – then we'll really need to talk – or play'.

It is possible for some therapeutic work relating to abuse to become polarised: either the child feels, through therapy, that eventually it will be all right in this family, people can be forgiven and the family can come together again OR the child is encouraged to express all the outrage and anger without any recognition of other feelings that may exist towards the abuser and those who failed to protect the child.

There are some family environments that are too toxic for children to live in – and children should not have to feel permanently guilty about leaving such families. In other cases, there are other families where repair is possible both for the child and for the family as a whole. This may turn out to be a 'good enough' family rather than an 'ideal' family, but it will be one where there is enough basic protection for the child.

Statements such as the one that Shaun made, are clear indications of why supervision is so important for the playtherapist's practice. When working with damaged children, it is all too easy to become involved in the child's experience and make judgements that are more to do with our own needs than with the child's needs. As an example of this, in the wish for a family to change and accommodate a distressed child, are we perhaps talking about *our own family* and the distress that we experienced as a child?

Renée's six-part story, using Lahad's BASIC Ph, showed a yearning to find the treasure 'with love hearts' on it which is thwarted by the pirate. However, the police will put Fred, the pirate, in jail.

Example

RENÉE'S SIX-PART STORY

1. HERO – Mickey Mouse, he has fluffy slippers on, and he lives at 17 Hill Road; he lives with his wife Minnie.

2. TASK – (Renée became quite animated, and looked lightened as if a load had been lifted from her shoulders.) His task is to find treasure, gold in a chest with a lock on it. There are golden necklaces with love hearts on them. The treasure is under a cave.

3. WHO CAN HELP? His wife Minnie can help him find the treasure, she spilt blood, no it's tomato sauce. Minnie has a wonderful golden dress.

4. WHAT OBSTACLES ARE IN THE WAY? Fred, a pirate, he has a covered up eye. He wants gold. He has a boat that says on it PIRATES ONLY.

5.   RESOLUTION. Mickey and Minnie bought a new house, and lived not
      very happily ever after with a new car. Their house is very small. They
      never found the treasure again.

If therapists feel outrage and indignation at the treatment of a child, is this
anger *on behalf of the child* or is it our own anger? Murray Cox's reminder to
therapists is very timely here – that we are *in* but not *of* the world of the
patient (Cox 1995).

   All children who come into therapy are, in their differing ways, in states of
shock and trauma. However, the child who has experienced sudden and
unexpected shock such as natural disasters, wars and serious crashes, has
particular needs.

Picture from Renée's six-part story

'Who can help?' by Renée

> It must be emphasised that stress is something determined subjectively by each individual according to assessment of the situation and past experiences. If the situation is translated as a threat to the individual, then stress will result. This threat need not necessarily be physical in nature, it could also be of three other basic types; a threat against one's family, friends or belongings; a threat against one's psychological integrity; and a threat against beliefs or values. (Lahad 1992)

We now understand more and more about post traumatic stress disorder (PTSD) in both children and adults. What is clear in the therapy offered in these situations is that explorations of the trauma are rarely the most effective way, certainly at the outset of therapy.

The threats or fear of threats against the individual as pointed out by Lahad, above, result in particular needs that have to be addressed. The following are usually the most immediate:

1. The person needs to develop the capacity to self-soothe; to nurture themselves. They have lost this ability through guilt ('I don't deserve to be cared for') or where there is actual loss of the carer (especially true for children).

2. The person needs to rediscover trusting relationship(s) which may begin in therapy and then generate out to other relationships. The therapist may well assist in that process through the symbolic play (see the case history of Penny below).

3. The person needs to find support as they live through the process of disillusionment and loss of belief that has been provoked by the trauma.

4. The person needs to externalise the trauma *in their own good time* – and not because the therapist thinks it may be a 'good thing'.

5. The person needs factual information – notice how important it was in the case of Penny below.

Example

Penny, aged eight, was formally referred for playtherapy following crisis-fostering after the sudden death of her parents in a road accident. The foster parents reported that she was quiet, good, did not talk, did everything she was told and answered any questions in monosyllables. She did not respond to any physical contact. The school had reported similarly: that she was well-behaved, carried out her work and did not join in playground games.

She came obediently into her playtherapy sessions, was shown all the materials, and responded 'yes, thank you' when asked if she understood what playtherapy was. Penny sat at the drawing table, took a pencil and paper, looked at the playtherapist and waited. The playtherapist suggested that she drew a garden and she produced the picture shown below. In response to being asked to describe her garden, she said 'There are the flowers, there is the grass, the sun is shining, there is a big tree – that's the gate to the garden'.

The inexperienced therapist might be tempted to charge right in and ask 'is the sun always shining?', thinking, quite rightly, that Penny has not been able to acknowledge when the sun set so tragically in her life. However, this would be premature – the key in this picture is the gate, as we shall see from the following intervention:

Penny's garden

'Tell me about the gate,' the therapist asked. Penny answered, 'The gate is locked – with a chain so that the garden stays safe – and then no one will spoil the flowers'. She then looked at the therapist for the first time and said, 'I want this garden to stay safe – and special'.

What multiple metaphoric expression is in this brief description – and the therapist is being told quite explicitly how to proceed. Don't open the gate – don't go into the garden – keep it *safe and special.* The garden is herself and also her past self when there were parents and life was secure – and maybe it is also linked to their graves – the healing metaphor at this point is the garden which is secure – not the garden to be invaded, spoiled or destroyed.

With the acknowledgement of the safe garden, Penny was able to express other things through different media. She constructed her foster family with the dolls' house and told a story about the 'new family' – 'and the old girl was sad to be in a new family because the old family had gone – but they were kind'.

Penny had been to the funeral and knew about the car accident – so it seemed appropriate for the therapist to say: 'and the old girl had had such a shock because the old family had gone so suddenly.' Penny looked at the therapist with fear in her eyes and said: 'they were crushed, weren't they?'

Although her parents had died instantly in a collision, it turned out that Penny had overheard someone say, 'they must have been crushed to death – the fire engine had to cut them out'.

The therapist is now wondering whether to follow the child into the everyday reality that Penny is describing, or to guide her back into the metaphoric reality of the story that Penny has been telling about the old and the new family.

The therapist said, 'The old girl is still shocked because no one exactly explained how the old Mummy and Daddy died'. (Penny slowly shook her head.) 'The old Mummy and Daddy died immediately the two cars crashed – and the cars had to be separated by the firemen – and the old girl was sad for a long time.' Penny answered with eyes full of tears: 'a long, long time.' (She put her head on her arms and started to cry.)

This example illustrates the many sub-texts that abound in such a situation and how the therapist *must* test the water with the child at each major step. In the situation above, the therapist chose to stay with the metaphor that the child had established in relation to 'the old family', 'the new family', and 'the old girl', and incorporated the fearful disclosure which, in turn, led into the first overt expression of grief.

Penny now began to ask questions about her parents' death from both her foster parents and her therapist; she gradually assimilated the real facts about their death. No one can minimise the effects of sudden death – especially to a child (Papadatou and Papadatos 1991). The next step for Penny was to be able to slowly work with her body and to allow physical touch; she was able to get into this through simple games in the soft area of the playroom and by choosing one special soft toy to play with as her 'new friend'. There were also stories about the old girl and the new friend. The foster parents got in touch to say that Penny would now allow herself to be tucked up in bed – to actually have the bedclothes tucked in round her – and had asked if she could have a duvet like the other children. This links with her earlier expression about being crushed and the fact that her avoidance of physicality seemed to have its dominant roots in physical fear.

In such cases, it is crucial that the child receives clear communication and explanations about what is happening which take into account the following:

- Has too much information been given too soon – especially if the child is in shock?

- How much information can the child retain at one go?

- What language is being used to explain things to the child? (Avoid adult logic or 'mimsy' language that dresses up the situation or avoids the real issues.)

- Who else has communicated to the child – have things been overheard and misunderstood?

- Has anyone tried to say to the child to 'forget all about it' when the child has not had time to mourn or grieve?

Children who have never been allowed or encouraged to play are quite overwhelmed when they come into a playtherapy situation (an example of this is the case history of Bobby, given in Chapter 5). Most rooms have so much choice and such a range of materials that a child can 'freeze' and be unable to begin.

It is important first to ascertain whether the child is unable to play because of developmental difficulties, due to early hospitalisation, for example, family trauma, or belief system, or whether there is organic damage which has impeded the usual learning stages. In cases where there is brain damage as well as prolonged hospitalisation, the play processes are likely to take that much longer.

> I was called into a Special Education Unit in eastern Europe to advise on play activities for children with brain damage; the existing equipment consisted of classical educational toys – wooden peg-boards; stacking shapes and rings; 'posting' shapes. Three girls sat at a table sorting glass beads into triangular sections in a round box. A younger boy, hyperactive, scampered around the room touching and dropping different equipment; he came to the table, grabbed a handful of beads – paused a moment – and flung them across the room, to the amusement of the three girls and the despair of the teacher.
>
> One bead had dropped on the table so I knelt down and blew it across to the other side of the table: the boy stopped in his tracks and watched: he then promptly moved opposite me and tried to blow the bead back. After several attempts he succeeded and we developed a simple game of

blowing the bead and then flicking the bead to each other; we then found it impossible to blow two beads at once, so we started lining the beads up according to their colour. The head teacher said that the boy had never been still since he had arrived at the school.

Many children are able to start at the beginning of their EPR stages and to work through them with the therapist taking care that the activities are age-appropriate in terms of preventing the children from feeling stupid. It is worth repeating that it is important not to bombard a child with stimulus. The situation can be contained within one small space – the table or the sandbox; or one medium – sand or plasticine; or one physical activity – rolling in different ways.

A child who is prevented from playing by the family who sees such activity as 'silly' or 'a waste of time', again needs a careful approach. The playtherapist is in effect giving permission for something that is not allowed at home and the child's value system will be in conflict. Peter Slade's guidelines (1954) for balancing the proportions of 'personal play and projective play' are important ones. Personal play involves the whole person – the child as actor is important for developing confidence and sociability; projective play, as well as being a medium for therapeutic expression, also enables the shy or withdrawn child to work safely within the technique and not take risks either physically or in role. Working in miniature can also be a way to engage with the reluctant child, using tiny toys or treasures.

The child who has not been allowed to play can be in a situation similar to that of the child who will not allow him or herself to play. With the former, the parents are exercising external control and in the latter the child is imposing internal control.

Yet another challenging situation arises with the very controlled child who is absolutely terrified of play and the seeming chaos that can result. It is important for the playtherapist not to impose a norm of playful behaviour but to allow for the individuality of the child within the range of diverse playing.

For the playtherapist, it is important to check out both the class and cultural norms regarding child development and play activity. Too often, for example, racial variation can be interpreted as pathology.

It is very easy to make assumptions in our practice. A nursery nurse student on placement chose to work with traveller children in a school near a traveller site. The student thought that playtherapy could be used to make the bridge between home and school and to express possible conflicts non-verbally. She arranged to work both with a small group of four children and with one child individually. In her supervision she was very distressed that all the children simply refused to play as she had expected and sat at the table wanting to do lessons. I suggested that she did some background work on traveller families before making any assumptions about the failure of the playtherapy. She discovered that traveller children who may well play freely out of doors, and be very inventive and creative with a whole range of media, are very different indoors. To them, the idea of taking off shoes and socks and sitting on the floor inside is anathema. This finding triggered a more detailed investigation into the complex set of rules and taboos surrounding the traveller belief system – one that is as complex as any other cultural or racial group.

Much of the Temiar data that I gathered in Malaysia made a lot of sense once I realised that the Temiar's spatial system is divided up into those activities that can take place on the ground and those that must take place off the ground (Jennings 1995c). Children are not allowed on the ground until they can walk independently. This is usually the time they are given their proper name – before they can walk they will have been known simply as 'boy' or 'girl'. From about the age of seven or eight, children no longer sleep near their parents but with their own peer group. Groups of seven- and eight-year-olds decide whose house they will sleep in on any particular evening. It was very difficult for me as a western mother to allow my own eight-year-old to sleep with his peer group in a different house and I always remember my own initial discomfort on these occasions as a guideline for not making assumptions about other cultures and belief systems. Equally, the playtherapist should always check what may be a perfectly ordinary explanation before assuming there is abnormality or disturbance: in other words, *ask the child.*

The playtherapist always has to balance the various factors before making assumptions about pathology and remember the story of the child sent for assessment who raced and jumped down stairs after going to the lavatory. When asked why he did it, he replied that he wanted to reach the bottom of the stairs before the water filled up again – in other words, this was a piece of play acting, a child's game.

If the child has recurring nightmares, the playtherapist should make sure to be clear about the development of anxiety (free floating) and fear (located). Parents should understand the various routines that can contain and change nightmare patterns. Children depend on the care of parents to survive so it is important that where possible the parents themselves can intervene to transform the fearful dream.

If a child comes to playtherapy because of nightmares it is important to start with an open contract, that is, the parents, therapist and child know why the child has come. The nightmare can be drawn and painted, modelled in plasticine or clay, or built in the sand tray with sand and water. It can be played out through the toys, through puppets and through dramatic play, and through story-telling. The child may need to move from one medium to another and to work the nightmare through in several ways. The child needs to find power to deal with the nightmare – to disempower the monster; the child may play the role of the monster, for example, in dramatic play. If the child draws a frightening monster together with a little child, progress to telling the story through the pictures. A nightmare may need to be worked at several times at intervals in order to bring about a decrease in its power. *If a nightmare persists after working through in therapy or if a new nightmare appears, check for other possibilities such as abuse.*

Among the range of playtherapy equipment, make sure you have plenty of monster toys – space monsters, prehistoric monsters, monster slime. Have very small versions of them too as a way for the child to take control and reduce their power. There are many stories about overcoming monsters, both old and new, that can be read, dramatised or modelled, as illustrated in Chapter 7.

Susan had a waking nightmares having read in an old book of her uncle's the story of Richard III murdering the little princes in the tower. She woke at night crying, and remembered much of the story verbatim, 'and the little princes looked like two pale flowers on the pillow'. She wanted her parents to destroy the book and when they demurred, made them lock it away in a cupboard. The book itself needed to be contained. The therapy consisted of a very brief intervention as she talked about how the story had frightened her, and how sorry she felt for the princes to be murdered by their uncle. I asked her directly if she was frightened of the uncle who had given her the book and she said that she wasn't but that she had never met him and didn't know who he was because the family did not approve of him.

Susan needed to talk through the story and her fear in daylight and to be able to understand her genuine feelings of grief at the death of these children through their very graphic story, together with the book's pictures. She was learning about the reality of death. She then asked for her book back because it represented an important link with this uncle she did not and would not know.

This chapter has dealt with some of the more difficult situations play-therapists may have to face in their work, and has addressed some of the realities of playtherapy in practice. Cross-cultural beliefs and racial variation have been commented upon. Suggestions have been made for working with more difficult problems, such as child abuse, the child who cannot or will not play, and the child who has nightmares. I stress again the importance of hearing the child and not making assumptions about interpretations.

Personal Reflection

As I approach what is euphemistically called 'riper years', I am even more convinced of the primacy of children's play for health and healing. A child who is able to play makes their own contribution to a healthy society, as well as having some chance of growing up to have an integrated personality and fulsome life.

If I have seemed to favour the 'hunter-gatherer' rather than the 'settled cultivator', that is my own gypsy sharing her preferences.

As a gypsy grandmother, I have had time to observe the play of my own grandchildren and to be ever enchanted by the wisdom in their view of the world.

This view of grandmothers by an eight-year-old boy is one of my treasures.

A grandmother is a woman who has no children of her own, and therefore she loves the boys and girls of other people. Grandmothers have nothing to do. They have only got to be there. If they take us for a walk they go slowly past beautiful leaves and caterpillars. They never say 'Come along quickly' or 'Hurry up for goodness sake'. They are usually fat, but not too fat to tie up our shoe strings. They wear spectacles and sometimes they can take out their teeth. They can answer every question, for instance why dogs hate cats and why God is not married. When they read to us they do not leave out anything and they do not mind if it is always the same story. Everyone should try to have a grandmother, 'specially those who have no television. Grandmothers are the only grown-ups who always have time.

'Why is God in Godzilla?' (Harry, aged four)

'Why is God in Godzilla?' (Harry, aged four)

Playtherapy Resources

Too often staff are asked to undertake playtherapy without consideration of such things as:

- environment: that is, the shape and size of room; floor covering; privacy
- time: for assessment and practice, as well as planning and recording
- media and materials, including range and choice
- supervision, consultation, support and training.

The following is an ideal requirement but consideration is also given to working with a modest budget and the provision of basic essentials which should not have to be compromised.

The Playtherapy Environment

A playtherapy space should be single purpose: warm, light and airy, with a view of the world beyond. Carpets are not advisable since they cause carpet burns during movement and do not give a child a feeling of immediate support. Woodblock or cork tiles are preferable, with non-slip mats in some areas. The room should be divided into several areas for different forms of play and have some larger equipment that is replaced as appropriate. The following are some examples:

- a soft area with a play mattress, cushions, pillows and blankets
- a wet area for sand and water play, with water, clay and mess
- a toy area for playing with different sorts of toys
- a drama area for games and drama
- a drawing and painting area with tables
- a quiet area for story-telling and reflection.

The soft area: a safe place for energetic physical games; jumping and rolling; hiding and sleeping. It can also be combined with the drama area (below) to create scenarios for enactment and dramatic play. It needs a number of soft toys and cushions of different shapes, sizes and colours that can be sat upon, built with, and used in a variety of ways during physical activities.

The wet area: needs a basin with hot and cold water, water and sand containers, a clay table and chairs.

The toy area: should have sturdy containers for different sets and groupings of toys; building materials and a dolls' house. Shelves may contain wooden boxes and plastic stacking bowls.

The drama area: this can be combined with the soft area and should have a simple climbing frame for creating houses or towers and a barrel to crawl into.

The drawing and painting area: should be near the wet area, with tables to sit or stand at for painting work.

The quiet area: this should be a calm and still area where a child can listen to a story; wind down from a session and reflect; or 'de-role' from the dramatic engagement before a session finishes. It needs a mat and cushions or chairs.

Interior Decoration

The walls of the playtherapy room need to be painted in light rather than bright colours, with a selection of posters and pictures that are not stereotypical or prejudicial in relation to gender, race or class. If the ceiling is high, an inexpensive false ceiling can be created with cross slats. Strip lighting should not be used. Concealed spotlights, which illuminate different areas in different ways, are the most appropriate. The room should also have sturdy, lockable cupboards for a child's own materials to be kept in. The main door should lock, but be able to be entered from the outside in emergencies; there should be an alarm system. The floor should be sealed to enable easy wiping and cleaning and to avoid the use of plastic covering.

When such a space is not available – as, for example, when a room is multi-purpose – then certain issues must be addressed. The room must then be available on a regular basis for therapy sessions, with sufficient time for preparation and clearing up. It must be private and not be part of a thoroughfare or have people knocking on the door or any other sort of interruption. However small the space, it should have contrasting areas even if these are simply a quiet area with an action area with water play in a washing-up bowl in one corner. Children's play-work which they wish to keep must have storage space that is locked and safe.

Ann Cattanach, one of my colleagues, spends some of her time working as a playtherapist *in situ*. She creates the space by taking with her a blue carpet (Cattanach 1992) and equipment in different sorts of bags. Whether the space is permanent or mobile, it must have the potential for creating a space that is different – a magical and symbolic space where things can be *allowed*. There are many feelings and thoughts that a child needs to feel safe to express and that cannot be expressed in any other space.

Media and Materials

With the plethora of play equipment available it is very difficult for playtherapists to be able to have a balanced range of equipment within their budget. It is important to check the following:

- Is the budget 'start-up' money (and therefore not to be repeated)?
- What about funding for consumables?
- Do other people have use of the equipment?
- Who is responsible for cleaning, tidying, mending and generally overseeing the equipment?
- Is there any variation in standards of maintenance? You may find that the way you maintain the equipment is different from other staff (rather as in families!) and this can cause friction and resentment.
- See if you can find a friendly printer who will allow you regular supplies of ends of rolls.
- Try not to confuse 'junk materials' for creating and exploring, with 'rubbish equipment' where everything is cracked, broken or has pieces missing.
- Be sure to check the safety standard, for example, toxicity of paint; eyes of soft toys; badly made toys; splinters; and so on.
- Make sure that there are aprons, old shirts and smocks in order to protect the child's personal clothing.

SOFT TOYS

Large, small, and very small soft, furry, cuddly toys (even teddy bears as big as a child) can be bought for under œ20. However, beware of fire hazards and cheap fur that can stick up noses and down throats and irritate eyes. Good fabric departments stock a large choice of fur fabrics from which many different toys can be made.

DOLLS' HOUSE

This should be an open-fronted dolls' house with a range of furniture that is as flexible as possible. There are wooden building sets that can be made into a dolls' house, as well as be turned into other buildings. You may want to have a second dolls' house which can be used for destructive/aggressive play. Beware of using stereotyped dolls.

SMALL ANIMALS

You can make a large collection of animals which include those on farms, zoos and those found in the wild. Include baby animals as well as adults and make sure there are land, water and air creatures. Include trees, gates, fences and cages as part of the collection.

TINY TOYS

The very small toys described in Chapter 6 come into this category, that is, a miniature Punch and Judy, nursery rhyme and fairy tale figures, etc. Tiny families (sleep dolls) can be found in charity shops or made from pipe cleaners. Baby animals can also be used here as well as magic 'jewels'.

EDUCATIONAL TOYS

A large range of wooden and plastic construction toys can be useful in the playtherapy room, especially to encourage mastery of skills and improve confidence. There is also a point where educational play coincides with therapeutic play and one experience leads to another.

WATER PLAY

A collection of useful objects includes a large water container with cups and saucers, funnels, sprays, feeding bottles and a water pistol.

SAND PLAY

Install a large container of sand (or use a tray or bowl), and use sand specifically refined for play. Sand may be mixed with water and used for building, tunnelling and decorating. Chapter 1 (pp.29, 30) includes a description of the particular forms of sand play used by Jungian child therapists, and particular use of sand play and toys can also be found in the 'World Technique' section of that chapter.

DRAWING AND PAINTING

Acquire a range of large 'jumbo' crayons, chrcoal and oil-based crayons, finger paint in primary colours, paints and large brushes and ample supplies of different sorts of paper.

JUNK PLAY

Collect cardboard boxes of all sizes (from fridge packaging to shoeboxes) for drama work and for creating 'journey boxes' or 'sense boxes'. Large boxes can become houses, castles and tunnels. They can also be built into totem poles, trees and bridges. Whole environments can be created from waste materials: shredded computer paper, newspaper, container rolls (although to use toilet roll middles is perhaps taking the notion of junk too far).

Fabric scraps of different textures and shapes are also useful; small pieces can be used for artwork/sculpting; larger pieces for dressing-up self and toys. Good quality material can be obtained from manufacturers and from the wardrobe departments of large theatres.

Leaves, twigs, grasses, straw and flowers can also be combined with sand play or used with other types of play materials.

NESTING DOLLS

Russian dolls (Babushkas) come in several shapes and sizes. Traditional-style peasant women with red headscarves are available and it is now possible to buy variations on this theme – ethnic dolls in saris and male as well as female doll sets.

PUPPETS

Glove and finger puppets are probably the most frequently used puppets in playtherapy. It is possible to obtain three-generational families of finger puppets and a variety of animals that are easy for small fingers to handle. Glove puppets can be made from gloves or socks, or from papier mfch, or fur fabric. Some puppets are too clumsy or heavy for small hands to manage.

Very small finger puppets can be used for 'tiny play' like other very small toys. A child can thus contain a whole family on the fingers of one hand.

DOLLS

Baby dolls can be used for bathing, dressing and undressing, and putting to bed. Other dolls can be used for family play. Some children prefer to work with dolls'-house-size dolls; others find that these are too tiny for easy use and choose to work in a larger dimension. The dolls can be combined with the soft toys for family and situation play and story-telling.

BOOKS

A range of suitable books can cover stories that can be used therapeutically as well as stories for health that can be read to children as part of the therapy. There are stories that can be painted, dramatised and improvised, and stories that can have new endings created for them. The playtherapist needs a rich fund of stories from their own experience to draw on and these should include stories from many different cultures.

MUSIC

Musical instruments are an important part of the playroom – bongo drums, cymbals, penny whistles and chime bars are essential basics and can be easily developed. Some playtherapists use taped music (and sound effects), but generally live music is preferable, particularly since many children are desensitised to music through experience of loud, non-stop, undifferentiated sound.

Developmental Checklist

Reproduced from *Drama in Therapy. Volume 1: Children* edited by R. Courtney and G. Schattner (1981).

0–3 months

  Skin and touch sensitivity
  Empathy with mother
  Mouth and hand play
  Sound repetition and vocal play
  Surprise at face

3–6 months

  Postural cues
  Movement repetition
  Interest in bodily things
  Interest in faces
  Interest in colours
  Play with food
  Play with toys
  Excitement at familiar things
  Laughs at surprise
  Moves and 'sings' with parent
  Crescendo ('This Little Piggy Went to Market')

6–12 months

  Crawling/walking
  Development of personal circle around body
  Pretends to be mother ('the primal act')
  Anticipates climax

Makes others audience
Clear purposes, goals
Demands attention
Repetitions
Sound games
Gestural language
Explores objects – realises their existence
Delight at outcome
'Peek-a-boo'
Jokes

1–2 years

Insatiable curiosity
Mischievousness
'Me' and 'mine'
Exchange with others
Words developing
Dances
Pretence actions
Makes toys pretend
Pretends objects are toys
Relates toys to one another (doll in another toy)
Makes exits and entrances
Carries treasures about
Crayons in fist
Being chased or chasing
Explorations: length/weight/number/size
Makes rules
Makes music in time, rhythm
Makes 'homes' (boxes, cloth)

2–3 years

Movement flexibility: speed, rhythm, up/down, front/back
Strategies (offers, bargains)
Running commentaries
Sentences develop
Complete sequences of action (time)
Personifies parent routines
Time: 'in a minute'/'in a little while'

Group choral games
Crayons in fingers
Joins toys in pretence
Changes roles
Narratives continued
Hide and seek/'house'/tag

3–4 years

'Why?'
Puzzles ('it fits')
Takes turns, sharing
Group games
Good gross motor control
Early grammar
Exaggerated stories
'Follow the leader'
Space differences made
Participates in narratives
Matching games (buttons/boxes)
Makes pretence environments
Runs from 'monsters'
dressing up
Pretence emotions
Groups of characters played
Acts problems/fairy stories

4–5 years

Fine motor control
Secrets, surprises
Grammar develops
Group pretence play
Early conscience
Friends and enemies
Seeks approval from peers
Highly imaginative roles
Different voices
Symbol distinguished from reality
Gymnastics
Free movement to music

Relay races/creeping
Pretends to tell the time
Games of order ('Ring around a Rosy')
Play rituals (possession, sequences)
Consciousness of roles of others
Puppets
Anticipates future
Invents narrative
Begins to learn to avoid aggression
Relies on own judgement

5–7 years

Learns time beat
Boy/girl/baby play (sex)
Group play
Groups move in large circles
Role flexibility
Social roles begun (teacher/pupil)
Caricature
Games of acceptance ('Farmer in the dell')
Playful conversations
Improvises movements, objects, characters, situations
Analogy/animism
Difficulty in distinguishing fantasy and reality
Makes costumes/clay models
Chasing and running games
Left/right awareness
Realistic themes
Episodic plots (picaresque)
Movement: 'big/small/grow'

7–9 years

Highly creative dance
Can write well
Play with mechanical toys
Collections, crazes, hobbies
Sense of fairness
Card and board games/creates own games
Feeling for ideas of others

Plays exaggerated roles
Distinguishes fantasy and reality
Plots: exaggerated/realistic/surprises/myths/legends/occupations
Establishes improved speech/rich flow/nonsense talk (gibberish)
Puppets and puppet theatres
Groups play in small circles/spirals
Games of dominance ('King of the castle')
Increased grace/speed
Large group improvisation/pairs/solos/leaders emerge
Ball games
Cumulative plots/long endings/abrupt finishes
Group play in horseshoe shape begun
Love of detail

9–13 years

Movement: changes in direction/focus/near and far
Increased clarity in gesture and body shape
Handicrafts
Very co-operative/independent
Winning/losing games
Intellectual games (charades)
Informal concerts
Growth of hypothesis/classification/historical sense
Small group improvisation/good partner work
Fluent speech
Language more important
Creative writing
Small scripts used in some improvisation
Invention of own languages
Use of private codes
Plots of climax and conflict
Themes: animals/adventure/occupations
Emotional characterisations
Social role playing increases/social playmaking
Increasing need to 'show'
Explores real in possible
Space: horseshoe shape developed/end shapes explored.

Role Skills and Expansion: Birth – Six Years (Sue Jennings)

- Imitation of sounds, gestures, reactions
- Innovation of new sounds, gestures, reactions
- Pretending to be adult, animal, monster
- Role-reversing with special toys
- Projective roles through objects
- Personifying family members or TV characters, with variation and not just replication
- Role-taking and the beginning of identification
- Enactment of roles and scenes with environments
- Dramatic play separated from other play activities
- Drama. All of the above and increased improvisation. Ideas are tested and repeated.

Bibliography

Aston Smith, J. (1993) *Alyson, The Story of a Green Witch.* Stratford-upon-Avon: SEJ publications.

Axline, V. (1964) *Dibs in Search of Self.* London: Penguin.

Axline, V. (1947/1969) Play Therapy. New York: Ballantino.

Bachelard, G. (1942) *Water and Dreams.* Dallas: Pegasus.

Bachelard, G. (1964) *The Poetics of Space.* Boston: Beacon Press.

Behar, D. and Rapaport, J.L. (1983) 'Play, observation and psychiatric diagnosis.' In C.E. Schaefer and K. O'Connor (eds) *Handbook of Playtherapy.* New York: John Wiley.

Booth, D. and Martin-Smith, A. (eds) (1988) *Re-Cognizing Richard Courtney.* Ontario: Pembroke Publishers.

Brook, P. (1988) *The Shifting Point.* London: Methuen.

Cambell, J. (1977) *The Hero with Two Thousand Faces.* New York: Bollingen.

Cattanach, A. (1992) *Play Therapy with Abused Children.* London: Jessica Kingsley Publishers.

Cattanach, A. (1994) *Play Therapy: Where the Sky Meets the Underworld.* London: Jessica Kingsley Publishers.

Cattanach, A. (1997) *Children's Stories in Play Therapy.* London: Jessica Kingsley Publishers.

Cook, R. (1974) *The Tree of Life.* London: Thames and Hudson.

Courtney, R. and Schattner, G. (eds) (1981) *Drama in Therapy. Volume 1: Children.* New York: Drama Book Specialists.

Courtney, R. (1982) *Re-Play.* Toronto: OISE Press.

Cox, M. (1995) *Structuring the Therapeutic Process: Compromise with Chaos – The Therapist's Response to the Individual and the Group.* London: Jessica Kingsley Publishers.

Crebbin, J. (1996) *Into the Castle.* London: Walker Books.

Dickens, C. (1987) *Oliver Twist.* Harmondsworth: Penguin.

Dickens, C. (1994) *Great Expectations.* Harmondsworth: Penguin.

Dickens, C. (1989) *Hard Times* (1854). Oxford: Oxford University Press.

Erikson, E. (1977) *Childhood in Society.* St Albans: Triad/Palladin.

Feilden, T. (1990) 'Art therapy as part of the world of dyslexic children.' In M. Liebmann (ed) *Art Therapy in Practice.* London: Jessica Kingsley Publishers.

Fordham, M. (1986) *Jungian Psychotherapy.* London: Maresfield.

Freud, S. (1922) *Beyond the Pleasure Principle.* London: Hogarth.

Gersie, A. and King, N. (1990) *Storymaking in Education and Therapy.* London: Jessica Kingsley Publishers.

Gersie, A. (1991) *Storymaking in Bereavement.* London: Jessica Kingsley Publishers.

Gersie, A. (1992) *Earth Tales.* London: Green Press.

Gersie, A. (ed) (1996) *Dramatic Approaches to Brief Therapy.* London: Jessica Kingsley Publishers.

Gersie, A. (1997) *Reflections on Therapeutic Storymaking: The Use of Stories in Groups.* London: Jessica Kingsley Publishers.

Gleitman, H. (1986) *Psychology.* New York: Norton.

Hollinghurst, H. (1973) *Gods and Heroes of Ancient Greece.* London: Heinemann Educational.

Horley, E. (1998) 'Developmental Assessment of Dramatic Play.' Paper presented to OMEP conference, Copenhagen, Denmark.

Huizinga, J. (1955) *Homo Ludens.* Boston: Beacon.

Hutchens, P. (1994) *The Very Worst Monster.* London: Bodley Head.

Irwin, E. (1983) 'The diagnostic and therapeutic use of pretend play.' In C.E. Schaefer and K. O'Connor (eds) *Handbook of Playtherapy.* New York: John Wiley.

Jacobson, E. (1964) *The Self and the Object World.* New York: International Universities Press.

James, H. (1991) *The Turn of the Screw (1854).* Toronto: Dover Thrift.

Jennings, S. (1972) *Video Drama with Disturbed Adolescents.* Buckingham: Open University Press.

Jennings, S. (1973)*Remedial Drama.* London: Pitman and AC Black.

Jennings, S. (1975) 'The importance of the body in non-verbal methods of therapy.' In S. Jennings (ed) *Creative Therapy.* Banbury: Kemble Press.

Jennings, S. (1977) 'Dramatherapy: the anomalous profession.' *Journal of Dramatherapy 4.*

Jennings, S. (1979) 'Ritual and the learning process.' *Journal of Dramatherapy 13,* 4.

Jennings, S. (1983a) 'Rites of healing.' Paper presented to Dramatherapy Conference, London.

Jennings, S. (1983b) 'The importance of social anthroplogy for therapists.' Talk given to Royal Anthropological Institute, London.

Jennings, S. (1985a) 'Temiar dance and the maintenance of order.' In P. Spencer (ed) *Society and the Dance.* Cambridge: Cambridge University Press.

Jennings, S. (1985b) 'The drama and the ritual, with reference to group analysis.' Paper presented to Spring Seminar Group Analytic Society.

Jennings, S. (1986a) *Creative Drama and Groupwork.* Bicester: Winslow Press.

Jennings, S. (1986b) 'Playing with ideas of play.' Paper presented to Art Therapy and Dramatherapy Summer School, St Albans.

Jennings, S. (1986c) 'The loneliness of the long distance therapist.' Paper presented to Jungian Summer Seminar.

Jennings, S. (1986d) 'Methaphors of violence.' Paper presented to International Congress of Group Psychotherapy, Zagreb.

Jennings, S. (ed) (1987) *Dramatherapy, Theory and Practice 1.* London: Routledge.

Jennings, S. (1990) *Dramatherapy with Families, Groups and Individuals.* London: Jessica Kingsley Publishers.

Jennings, S. (1992a) *Dramatherapy Theory and Practice 2*. London: Routledge.

Jennings, S. (1992b) 'The nature and scope of dramatherapy: Theatre of healing.' In M. Cox (ed) *Shakespeare Comes to Broadmoor*. London: Jessica Kingsley Publishers.

Jennings, S. (1993) *Play Therapy with Children: A Practitioner's Guide*. Oxford: Blackwell Scientific.

Jennings, S. (1994) 'Unravelling dramatherapy: Ariadne's ball of thread.' *Family Context*.

Jennings, S. (1994) 'The theatre of healing; metaphor and metaphysics in the healing process.' In S. Jennings, A. Cattanach, S. Mitchell, A. Chesner and R. Meldrum (eds) *The Handbook of Dramatherapy*. London: Routledge.

Jennings, S. (ed) (1995a) *Infertility Counselling*. Oxford: Blackwell Science.

Jennings, S. (ed) (1995b) *Dramatherapy with Children and Adolescents*. London: Routledge.

Jennings, S. (1995c) *Theatre Ritual and Transformation*. London: Routledge.

Jennings, S. (1996) *Brief dramatherapy – the healing power of the dramatized here and now.'* In Alida Gersie (ed) *Dramatic Approaches to Brief Therapy*. London: Jessica Kingsley Publishers.

Jennings, S. (ed) (1997) *Dramatherapy Theory and Practice 3*. London: Routledge.

Jennings, S. (in preparation) *The Theatres of Healing*. London: Jessica Kingsley Publishers.

Jennings, S. and Minde, A. (1994) *Art Therapy and Dramatherapy: Masks of The Soul*. London: Jessica Kingsley Publishers.

Jennings, S. (1998) *Introduction to Dramatherapy*. London: Jessica Kingsley Publishers.

Jennings, S. (1999, in press) 'EPR for actors.' *Journal of Dramatherapy*.

Kalff, D. (1980) *Sandplay*. Santa Monica: Sigo Press.

Kernberg, O. (1984) *Object-Relations Theory and Clinical Psychoanalysis*. New York: Jason Aronson.

Klein, M. (1932) *The Psychoanalysis of Children*. London: Hogarth.

Lahad, M. (1987) *Community Stress Prevention*. Israel: Kyriat Shmona.

Lahad, M. (1992) 'Story-making and assessment method for coping with stress: Six-piece story and BASIC Ph.' *Dramatherapy Theory and Practice 2*. London: Routledge.

Landy, R. (1993) *Persona and Performance – The Meaning of Role in Drama, Therapy and Everyday Life*. London: Jessica Kingsley Publishers.

Landy, R. (1996) *Essays in Drama Therapy: The Double Life*. London: Jessica Kingsley Publishers.

Lowenfeld, M. (1935) *Play in Childhood*. London: Mackeith Press.

Masson, J. (1997) *Dogs Never Lie About Love*. London: Vintage.

Miller, A. (1990) *The Untouched Key*. London: Virago Press.

Miller, A. (1983) *For Your Own Good*. London: Faber.

Neumann, E. (1973) *The Child*. London: Hodder and Stoughton.

Oaklander, V. (1978) *Windows to our Children*. Utah: Real People Press.

Papadatou, D. and Papadatos, C. (1991) (eds) *Children and Death*. London: Hemisphere.

Piaget, J. (1962) *Play, Dreams, and Imitation in Childhood*. London: Routledge.

Radice, B. (1971) *Who's Who in the Ancient World*. Harmondsworth: Penguin.

Rycroft, C. (1985) *Psychoanalysis and Beyond*. London: Chatto.

Schlicke, P. (1989) 'Introduction to *Hard Times.*' Oxford: Oxford World's Classics.

Sherborne, V. (1975) *Movement with Mentally Handicapped Children in Creative Therapy.* London: Pitman.

Sherborne, V. (1990) *Developmental Movement for Children.* Cambridge: CUP.

Slade, P. (1954) *Child Drama.* London: Hodder and Stoughton.

Smilonsky, S. (1968) *The Effects of Sociodramatic Play on Disadvantaged Pre-School Children.* New York: John Wiley.

Trevarthen, C. and Logotheti, T. (1989) 'Child in society, and society in children: The nature of baisc trust.' in S. Howell and R. Willis (eds) *Societies at Peace: Anthropological Perspectives.* London: Routledge.

Winnicott, D.W. (1974) *Playing and Reality.* London: Pelican.

Winnicott, D.W. (1975) *Through Paediatrics to Psychoanalysis.* London: Hogarth.

Subject Index

Author Index